TINY TRAINS

A Guide to Britain's Miniature Railways 2007-2008

EDITOR
John Robinson

First Edition

ACKNOWLEDGEMENTS

We were greatly impressed by the friendly and cooperative manner of the staff and helpers of the railways and societies which we selected to appear in this book, and wish to thank them all for the help they have given. In addition we wish to thank Bob Budd (cover design) and Michael Robinson (page layouts) for their help.

We are particularly indebted to Peter Bryant for his invaluable assistance. Peter's web site: www.miniaturerailwayworld.co.uk provides a great deal of information about Miniature Railways in the UK.

Although we believe that the information contained in this guide is accurate at the time of going to press, we, and the Railways and Societies itemised, are unable to accept liability for any loss, damage, distress or injury suffered as a result of any inaccuracies. Furthermore, we and the Societies are unable to guarantee operating and opening times which may always be subject to cancellation without notice.

If you feel we should include other locations or information in future editions, please let us know so that we may give them consideration.

John Robinson

John Robinson

EDITOR

British Library Cataloguing in Publication Data
A catalogue record for this book is available from the British Library

ISBN-13: 978-1-86223-157-3

Copyright © 2007, MARKSMAN PUBLICATIONS. (01472 696226)
72 St. Peter's Avenue, Cleethorpes, N.E. Lincolnshire, DN35 8HU, England

Manufactured in the UK by LPPS Ltd, Wellingborough, NN8 3PJ

COVER PHOTOGRAPH

This features 'Jean' and was taken at the Brookside Miniature Railway in Poynton on 24th February 2007.

CONTENTS

THE FRIENDS OF THE NATIONAL RAILWAY MUSEUM

This organisation was formed in 1977 to help conserve and operate railway exhibits that might otherwise have to wait many years before returning to public view. The organisation is run on a membership basis which imparts a number of privileges which include:

* the *NRM Review*, published quarterly, which keeps Friends in touch with events at the Museum, carries information about the National Collection locomotives, features articles of general railway interest and includes authorative reviews of videos and books.

* opportunities to work as a volunteer in the Museum.

* invitations to FNRM members meetings in York and London.

MEMBERSHIP DETAILS – Normal membership is valid for 12 months from date of registration.

Category	Rate	
Ordinary	£20.00	Apply for membership to:
Unwaged	£15.00	**FNRM**
Junior (Under 18)	£10.00	**National Railway Museum**
Family/Couple	£30.00	**Leeman Road**
Retired Couple	£22.50	**York**
Group	£35.00	**YO26 4XJ**
Life (below 60)	£300.00	
Life (60 and over)	£225.00	**Telephone (01904) 636874**
Life (retired couple)	£350.00	**e-mail fnrm@nmsi.ac.uk**
Life (family)	£450.00	

Family Membership – is for a maximum of four persons, two or three of whom are under 18 years of age, residing at the same address

Retired Couple Membership – is for two persons aged 60 or over and not in employment.

NATIONAL RAILWAY MUSEUM

Address: National Railway Museum, Leeman Road, York YO26 4XJ **Telephone Nº**: 0870 421-4001 **Fax Nº**: (01904) 611112 **E-mail**: nrm@nrm.org.uk **Web site**: www.nrm.org.uk	**Year Formed**: 1975 **Location of Line**: York **Length of Line**: Short demonstration line **Nº of Steam Locos**: 79 **Nº of Other Locos**: 37 **Approx Nº of Visitors P.A.**: 800,000

GENERAL INFORMATION

Nearest Mainline Station: York (¼ mile)
Nearest Bus Station: York (¼ mile)
Car Parking: On site car park (£7.00 per day)
Coach Parking: On site – free to pre-booked groups
Souvenir Shop(s): Yes
Food & Drinks: Yes

SPECIAL INFORMATION

The Museum is the largest of its kind in the world, housing the Nation's collection of locomotives, carriages, uniforms, posters and an extensive photographic archive. Special events and exhibitions run throughout the year. The Museum is the home of the Mallard – the fastest steam locomotive in the world and Shinkansen, the only Bullet train outside of Japan.

OPERATING INFORMATION

Opening Times: Open daily 10.00am to 6.00pm (closed on 24th, 25th and 26th of December)
Steam Working: School holidays – please phone to confirm details
Prices: Free admission for all (excludes some Special events)
Phone (01904) 686263 for further details.

Detailed Directions by Car:
The Museum is located in the centre of York, just behind the Railway Station. It is clearly signposted from all approaches to York.

Shildon is one of the world's oldest railway towns and was selected by the National Railway Museum as a site for Locomotion, the first national museum to be built in the North East. The new building houses the reserve collection of historically important railway vehicles and these are now accessible to the public for the first time.

Shildon was home to the Timothy Hackworth Museum with its workshops and historic buildings and the incorporation of these with the new Locomotion museum creates an exciting opportunity to discover the significance of Shildon in railway history.

The replica Sans Pareil locomotive pictured below gives rides during the Summer School Holidays and on other special event days.

LOCOMOTION – THE NATIONAL RAILWAY MUSEUM AT SHILDON

Address: Locomotion, Shildon, County Durham   DL14 1PQ
Telephone Nº: (01388) 777999
Fax Nº: (01388) 771448
Year Formed: 2004
Location: Shildon, County Durham

Length of Line: Over ½ mile
Nº of Steam Locos: 60 locomotives and other rail vehicles
Approx Nº of Visitors P.A.: 60,000+
Gauge: Standard
Web site: www.locomotion.uk.com

GENERAL INFORMATION

Nearest Mainline Station: Shildon (adjacent)
Nearest Bus Station: Durham
Car Parking: Available on site
Coach Parking: Available on site
Souvenir Shop(s): Yes
Food & Drinks: Yes

SPECIAL INFORMATION

This extensive site is the first regional branch of the National Railway Museum and houses vehicles from the National Collection in a purpose-built 6,000 square-foot building.

OPERATING INFORMATION

Opening Times: Daily from 27th May 2007 to 30th September 2007 – 10.00am to 5.00pm. Also open from Wednesday to Sunday during the Winter season – 1st October to 1st April from 10.00am to 4.00pm although the Museum is closed over the Christmas and New Year Holiday period.
Steam Working: During the Summer School Holidays and on special event days – please phone to confirm details.
Prices: Free admission for all.

Detailed Directions by Car:
From All Parts: Exit the A1(M) at Junction 58 and take the A68 and the A6072 to Shildon. Follow the Brown tourist signs to Locomotion which is situated ¼ mile to the south-east of the Town Centre.

RAILWAY LOCATOR MAP

The numbers shown on this map relate to the page numbers for each railway. Pages 3-5 contain an alphabetical listing of the railways featured in this guide. Please note that the markers on this map show the approximate location only.

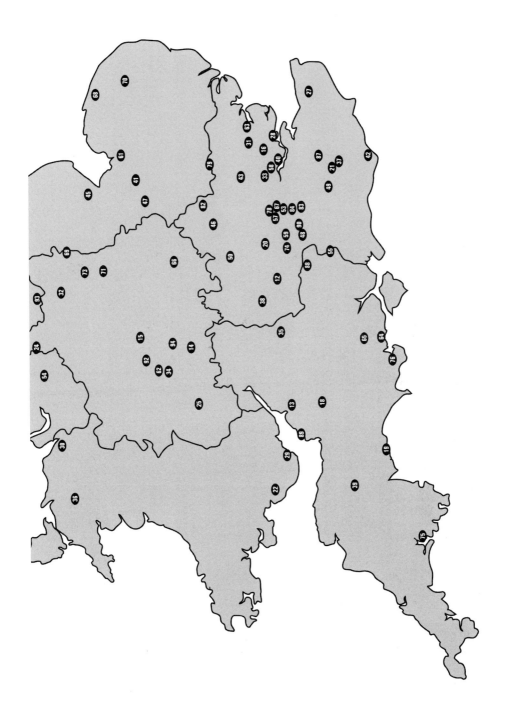

AMNERFIELD MINIATURE RAILWAY

Address: Amners Farm, Burghfield, Berkshire
Telephone N°: (0118) 970-0274
Year Formed: 1995
Location of Line: Amners Farm
Length of Line: ¾ mile

N° of Steam Locos: 3
N° of Other Locos: 3
N° of Members: 9
Approx N° of Visitors P.A.: 1,000
Gauge: 5 inches and 7¼ inches

GENERAL INFORMATION

Nearest Mainline Station: Theale (2 miles)
Nearest Bus Station: Reading
Car Parking: Free parking available on site
Coach Parking: None
Souvenir Shop(s): None
Food & Drinks: Available

OPERATING INFORMATION

Opening Times: Easter Sunday then the fourth Sunday in each month from April to October. Trains run from 2.00pm to 5.00pm
Steam Working: Every operating day.
Prices: Adults £1.00
Concessions 50p
Family Ticket £4.00

Detailed Directions by Car:
From All Parts: Exit the M4 at Junction 12 and take the A4 towards Reading. After approximately 2 miles turn right at the traffic lights into Burghfield Road. Continue along this road passing over the motorway then take the first turning on the left into Amners Farm Road. After approximately ½ mile turn right into Amners Farm.

Ashton Court Estate Miniature Railway

Address: Ashton Court Estate, Long Ashton, North Somerset BS41 9JN
Telephone Nº: (0117) 963-9174
Year Formed: Opened 1973
Location of Line: Ashton Court Estate
Length of Line: Two tracks, each approximately 1 mile in length

Nº of Steam Locos: 2
Nº of Other Locos: 2
Nº of Members: 240
Approx Nº of Visitors P.A.: 30,000
Gauge: 5 inches and 7¼ inches
Web site: www.bristolmodelengineers.co.uk

GENERAL INFORMATION

Nearest Mainline Station: Bristol Temple Meads (Approximately 5 miles)
Nearest Bus Station: Bristol (4 miles)
Car Parking: Free parking available on site
Coach Parking: Available by prior arrangement
Souvenir Shop(s): None
Food & Drinks: None

SPECIAL INFORMATION

The Railway is owned and operated by the Bristol Society of Model & Experimental Engineers which was founded in 1909.

OPERATING INFORMATION

Opening Times: Bank Holidays and some Sundays between April and mid-October (22 public passenger carrying days per year). Please contact the railway for a list of dates. On operating days, trains run from 12.00pm to 5.15pm.
Steam Working: All operating days.
Prices: 50p per ride per person.

Detailed Directions by Car:
Exit the M5 at junction 19 and take the A369 towards Bristol. After approximately 6 miles, just past the B3129 traffic lights is Ashton Court Estate. However, there is no right turn from this direction. Instead, take the side road on the left (North Road), turn right into Bridge Road and continue straight across the A369 at the traffic lights into the Clifton Lodge Entrance. Take the first right then the first right again before the golf kiosk car park.

Avonvale Model Engineering Society

Address: Hillers, Dunnington, Warwickshire B49 5PD	**N° of Steam Locos**: 12
Phone N°: (01242) 675219 (Secretary)	**N° of Other Locos**: 10
Year Formed: 2001	**N° of Members**: Approximately 40
Location of Line: Hillers, Dunnington	**Approx N° of Visitors P.A.**: 3,000
Length of Line: A third of a mile	**Gauge**: 5 inches and 7¼ inches

GENERAL INFORMATION

Nearest Mainline Station: Evesham (11 miles)
Nearest Bus Station: Stratford-upon-Avon (13 miles)
Car Parking: Free parking available on site
Coach Parking: None
Souvenir Shop(s): None
Food & Drinks: Available

SPECIAL INFORMATION

The Engines are all privately owned and run as required. The railway is located at Hillers where other attractions include a Café, a Farm Shop and a Display Garden.

OPERATING INFORMATION

Opening Times: All Bank Holiday Mondays and also on two other weekends per month from April to October. Please contact the railway for details about operating dates and times.
Steam Working: Where possible at least two steam locos run on each operating day.
Prices: 70p per ride per person.

Detailed Directions by Car:
From the North: Take the A435 or A46 to Alcester then follow the B4088 to Dunnington. Once in Dunnington, turn right at the crossroad and Hillers is on the right hand side with the railway visible from the road; From the South: Take the Evesham bypass then follow the B4088 to Dunnington.

BALLENY GREEN RAILWAY

Address: Balleny Green, Little Hay Lane, Little Hay WS14 0QB	**N° of Steam Locos**: 20 (approximately)
Telephone N°: (0121) 378-3992	**N° of Other Locos**: 4
Year Formed: 1948	**N° of Members**: Approximately 120
Location of Line: To the North of Little Hay Hamlet	**Approx N° of Visitors P.A.**: 4,500
Length of Line: One third of a mile	**Gauge**: 2½ inches, 3½ inches, 5 inches and 7¼ inches
	Web site: www.scmes.freeserve.co.uk

GENERAL INFORMATION

Nearest Mainline Station: Blake Street (1½ miles)
Nearest Bus Station: Sutton Coldfield (5 miles)
Car Parking: Available on site
Coach Parking: None
Food & Drinks: Drinks available at all times with food available at some special events

SPECIAL INFORMATION

The Railway is operated by members of the Sutton Coldfield Model Engineering Society and has been based at Balleny Green since 1981. The site has been progressively developed since this date.

OPERATING INFORMATION

Opening Times: Some Saturdays, Sundays and Bank Holidays throughout the year. Also at various other dates. Please contact the Society or check their web site for further details.
Steam Working: All operating days.
Prices: Prices depend on the event being held.

Detailed Directions by Car:
From the A38/A5 Junction: Head south on the A38 dual carriageway and turn right at the sign for Little Hay. Follow the road past the Pumping Station and after ¼ mile turn left through the steel gates set in stone columns with lanterns to enter the railway. Continue over the level crossing and turn right for the car park.

BARLEYLANDS MINIATURE RAILWAY

Address: Barleylands, Barleylands Road, Billericay, Essex CM11 2UD
Telephone Nº: (01268) 290229
Year Formed: 1989
Location of Line: 3 miles from Billericay
Length of Line: ½ mile
Web site: www.barleylands.co.uk

Nº of Steam Locos: 6
Nº of Other Locos: 2
Nº of Members: None
Annual Membership Fee: –
Approx Nº of Visitors P.A.: 10,000+
Gauge: 7¼ inches

GENERAL INFORMATION

Nearest Mainline Station: Billericay or Basildon
Nearest Bus Station: Billericay or Basildon
Car Parking: Available on site
Coach Parking: Available on site
Souvenir Shop(s): Yes
Food & Drinks: Yes

SPECIAL INFORMATION

The Railway is located in the Barleylands Craft Village and Farm Centre which has a wide range of attractions for all ages. The railway is commercially operated but volunteers help to operate and maintain the steam engines.

OPERATING INFORMATION

Opening Times: Daily from March to October with Santa Specials in December.
Steam Working: Sundays and Bank Holidays then daily (except Saturdays) in August and October Half-Term week. Also at a number of other special events throughout the year. Please phone the railway to confirm all running dates.
Prices: £1.00 Return (all ages) when Diesel-hauled
 £1.50 Return (all ages) when Steam-hauled

Detailed Directions by Car:
From M25: Exit at J29 onto A127 (Southend bound) and follow the brown Tourist Information signs for Farm Museum; From the A12: Take the B1007 Billericay junction, towards Stock and follow the brown Tourist Information signs for Farm Museum.

BARNSLEY SOCIETY OF MODEL ENGINEERS

Address: Park Mill Way, Clayton West,
near Huddersfield, W. Yorks.   HD8 9XJ
Phone Nº: (01226) 763731 (Secretary)
Year Formed: 1955
Location of Line: Kirklees Light Railway,
Clayton West
Length of Line: Approximately 650 feet

Nº of Steam Locos: 20
Nº of Other Locos: 4
Nº of Members: 26
Annual Membership Fee: £1.00
Approx Nº of Visitors P.A.: 4,000
Gauges: 3½ inches, 5 inches & 7¼ inches

GENERAL INFORMATION

Nearest Mainline Station: Denby Dale (4 miles)
Nearest Bus Station: Bus stop outside gates. Take
the 484 from Wakefield or the 235 and 240 from
Huddersfield/Barnsley.
Car Parking: Ample free parking at site
Coach Parking: Ample free parking at site
Souvenir Shop(s): Yes
Food & Drinks: Yes

SPECIAL INFORMATION

The Barnsley S.M.E. track is sited at the Kirklees
Light Railway.

OPERATING INFORMATION

Opening Times: Trains run from 11.00am to
5.00pm on Saturdays.
Steam Working: All operating days.
Prices: 50p per ride.

Detailed Directions by Car:
The Railway is located on the A636 Wakefield to Denby Dale road. Turn off the M1 at Junction 39 and follow the
A636 signposted for Denby Dale. Continue for approximately 4 miles then the railway is on the left after passing
under the railway bridge and is situated at the top of the Industrial Estate, just before the village of Scissett.

BATH & WEST RAILWAY

Address: The Royal Bath and West Showground, Shepton Mallet, Somerset, BA4 6QN
Phone N°: (01749) 840368 (Secretary)
Year Formed: 2001
Length of Line: 550 metres at present

N° of Steam Locos: 2
N° of Other Locos: 2
N° of Members: Approximately 60
Annual Membership Fee: £25.00
Approx N° of Visitors P.A.: 8,000
Gauge: 5 inches and 7¼ inches
Web site: www.essmee.org.uk

GENERAL INFORMATION

Nearest Mainline Station: Castle Cary (4 miles)
Nearest Bus Station: –
Car Parking: Free parking available on site
Coach Parking: Available
Food & Drinks: Available

SPECIAL INFORMATION

The Bath & West Railway is operated by members of the East Somerset Society of Model and Experimental Engineers.

OPERATING INFORMATION

Opening Times: As the railway is situated on The Royal Bath and West Showground, operating days are governed by public access to the site. The railway operates on the four days of the Royal Bath & West Show at the end of May and the three days of The National Amateur Gardening Show early in September. Organisers of other shows have also asked the Society to operate the railway during their shows so please contact the Society for further dates.
Steam Working: All operating days.
Prices: £1.00 per ride per person. Please note that additional fees may have to be paid by members of the public to gain entrance to the shows.

Detailed Directions by Car:
From All Parts: The Royal Bath and West Showground is situated approximately 2 miles south of Shepton Mallet just off the A371 road to Castle Cary.

Beer Heights Light Railway

Address: Pecorama, Beer, East Devon, EX12 3NA	**N° of Steam Locos**: 7 at present
Telephone N°: (01297) 21542	**N° of Other Locos**: 2
Year Formed: 1975	**N° of Members**: –
Location of Line: Beer, East Devon	**Approx N° of Visitors P.A.**: 60,000
Length of Line: 1 mile	**Gauge**: 7¼ inches
	Web site: www.peco-uk.com

GENERAL INFORMATION

Nearest Mainline Station: Axminster
Nearest Bus Station: Beer
Car Parking: Available on site
Coach Parking: Available on site
Souvenir Shop(s): Yes
Food & Drinks: Licensed restaurant on site

SPECIAL INFORMATION

In addition to the Railway, Pecorama features a Model Railway Exhibition, childrens activity areas and extensive gardens.

OPERATING INFORMATION

Opening Times: Weekdays 10.00am to 5.30pm and Saturdays 10.00am to 1.00pm from Easter to the end of October. Also open on Sundays from Whitsun to the start of September from 10.00am to 5.30pm
Steam Working: Daily
Prices: Adult £6.00
    Child £4.00 (Under-4s free of charge)
    Senior Citizens £5.50 (Over-80s free)
Entrance to Pecorama includes one ride on the railway in the price.

Detailed Directions by Car:
From All Parts: Take the A3052 to Beer, turn onto the B3174 and follow the Brown Tourist signs for Pecorama.

Bekonscot Light Railway

Address: Bekonscot Model Village, Warwick Road, Beaconsfield, Bucks, HP9 2PL
Telephone No: (01494) 672919
Year Formed: 2001
Location of Line: Beaconsfield, Bucks.
Length of Line: 400 yards

No of Steam Locos: None at present
No of Other Locos: 3
No of Members: –
Approx No of Visitors P.A.: 180,000
Gauge: 7¼ inches
Web site: www.bekonscot.com

GENERAL INFORMATION
Nearest Mainline Station: Beaconsfield (5 minutes walk)
Nearest Bus Station: High Wycombe
Car Parking: Available on site
Coach Parking: Available on site
Souvenir Shop(s): Yes
Food & Drinks: Available

SPECIAL INFORMATION
The Railway is situated in Bekonscot Model Village, a 1½ acre miniature landscape of fields, farms, castles, churches, woods and lakes which also contains a model railway.

OPERATING INFORMATION
Opening Times: Daily from mid-February to the end of October. Open 10.00am to 5.00pm.
Steam Working: None at present
Prices: Adult £6.50
Child £4.00
Family Ticket £19.00
Senior Citizen £4.50

Detailed Directions by Car:
From All Parts: Exit the M40 at Junction 2 taking the A355 then follow the signs for the "Model Village".

BOLEBROKE CASTLE & LAKES STEAM RAILWAY

Address: Bolebroke Castle, Edenbridge Road, Hartfield, East Sussex   TN7 4JJ
Telephone Nº: (01892) 770061
Year Formed: 1984
Location of Line: Bolebroke Castle
Length of Line: ½ mile

Nº of Steam Locos: 7
Nº of Other Locos: 8
Nº of Members: Approximately 36
Annual Membership Fee: £15.00
Approx Nº of Visitors P.A.: –
Gauge: 7¼ inches

GENERAL INFORMATION

Nearest Mainline Station: Tunbridge Wells
Nearest Bus Station: Hartfield
Car Parking: Available on site
Coach Parking: Available on site
Souvenir Shop(s): Yes
Food & Drinks: Yes

SPECIAL INFORMATION

The Railway runs around a lake situated in the grounds of a historic 15th Century Castle. Entrance to the castle is restricted so please phone for details of opening times.

OPERATING INFORMATION

Opening Times: Weekends from April to October and daily during the School holidays.
Steam Working: Some Sundays – phone for details
Prices: Admission to the grounds of the castle is free of charge. Admission prices for the castle itself are: Adult £5.00
        Child £2.50
        Senior Citizen £4.50

Detailed Directions by Car:
From All Parts: Take the A264 from Tunbridge Wells towards East Grinstead and turn off for Hartfield on either the B2110 (via Groombridge) or the B2026. Follow signs for Bolebroke Castle for the railway.

BRIDGEND & DISTRICT M.E.S.

Address: Fountain Road, Tondu, Bridgend
Telephone N°: None
Year Formed: 1984
Location of Line: Tondu, near Bridgend
Length of Line: –

N° of Steam Locos: 6
N° of Other Locos: 6
N° of Members: Approximately 35
Approx N° of Visitors P.A.: 800
Gauge: 3½ inches, 5 inches & 7¼ inches

GENERAL INFORMATION

Nearest Mainline Station: Tondu (1 mile)
Nearest Bus Station: Bridgend (2 miles)
Car Parking: Available on site
Coach Parking: Available on site
Food & Drinks: Available

OPERATING INFORMATION

Opening Times: The first Saturday of every month from April to October inclusive. Also on various other special open days. Please contact the railway for further details. Trains run from noon until 5.00pm.
Steam Working: All open days and most operating Saturdays.
Prices: 50p per person per ride.

Detailed Directions by Car:
Exit the M4 at Junction 36 and follow the A4063 Northwards. At the first roundabout take the 2nd exit onto the B4281 Park Road. Continue into Fountain Road and turn right (still on Fountain Road). The MES club area is located on the right just before the crossroads.

Brighouse & Halifax Model Engineers

Address: Ravensprings Park, Cawcliffe Road, Brighouse HD6 2HP
Telephone Nº: (01484) 710672
Year Formed: 1932
Location of Line: Ravensprings Park
Length of Line: 650 feet (5 inch gauge) and 1,200 feet (7¼ inch gauge)

Nº of Steam Locos: 50-60
Nº of Other Locos: 2 (traction engines)
Nº of Members: Approximately 75
Approx Nº of Visitors P.A.: 4,500
Gauge: 2½ inches, 3½ inches, 5 inches and 7¼ inches

GENERAL INFORMATION

Nearest Mainline Station: Brighouse (1½ miles)
Nearest Bus Station: Brighouse (1 mile)
Car Parking: Available on site
Coach Parking: Available by prior arrangement
Food & Drinks: Available on open days

OPERATING INFORMATION

Opening Times: Open to the public on the second Sunday of each month from April to October inclusive plus Santa Specials on 8th & 9th December 2007 (bookings essential for Santa Specials). Trains run from 1.30pm to 5.00pm.
Steam Working: All operating days.
Prices: Adults £2.50 (unlimited rides)
              Children £1.50 (unlimited rides)

Detailed Directions by Car:
Ravensprings Park lies in the Northern part of Brighouse. From the South: Take the A641 Bradford Road northwards and turn left just after The Martin's Nest Public House into Cross Street for Smith Carr Lane. Turn right into Bracken Road then left into Cawcliffe Road for the Park; From the North: Travel into Brighouse on the A641 and turn right just before The Martin's Nest Public House into Cross Street. Then as above.

BROOKSIDE MINIATURE RAILWAY

Address: Macclesfield Road (A523), Poynton, Cheshire SK12 1BY	**Nº of Steam Locos**: 5
Telephone Nº: (01625) 872919	**Nº of Other Locos**: 3
Year Formed: 1989	**Nº of Members**: –
Location: Brookside Garden Centre	**Approx Nº of Visitors P.A.**: 120,000
Length of Line: Approximately ½ mile	**Gauge**: 7¼ inches
	Web: www.brookside-miniature-railway.co.uk

GENERAL INFORMATION

Nearest Mainline Station: Poynton and Hazel Grove (both 1 mile)
Nearest Bus Station: Stockport (5 miles).
Car Parking: 400 spaces available on site
Coach Parking: 2 spaces available
Souvenir Shop(s): Yes
Food & Drinks: Yes

SPECIAL INFORMATION

The Railway runs through the grounds of the Brookside Garden Centre. There is also an extensive collection of Railwayana on display.

OPERATING INFORMATION

Opening Times: Railway is open weekends and Bank Holidays plus Wednesdays from March to September. Open every day in July and August. Trains usually run from 10.45am to 4.30pm but only until 4.00pm from November to February.
Steam Working: Weekends and Bank Holidays only
Prices: Adult £1.30 per ride (10 ride tickets £10.00)
          Child £1.30 per ride (10 ride tickets £10.00)
Note: Under-2s ride for free

Detailed Directions by Car:
From the North: Exit the M60 at Junction 1 in Stockport and take the A6 (signposted Buxton). Upon reaching Hazel Grove, take the A523 to Poynton. Follow the brown tourist signs for the Railway; From the West: Exit the M56 at Junction 6 signposted Wilmslow and continue to Poynton. Follow the brown signs for the Railway; From the South: Exit the M6 at Junction 18 for Holmes Chapel. Follow the signs to Wilmslow, then as from the West; From the East: Follow the A6 to Hazel Grove, then as from the North.

BROOMY HILL RAILWAY

Address: Broomy Hill, Hereford	**N° of Steam Locos**: 4+
Telephone N°: (01989) 762119	**N° of Other Locos**: 1+
Year Formed: 1962	**N° of Members**: Approximately 80
Location of Line: Adjacent to the	**Approx N° of Visitors P.A.**: Not known
Waterworks Museum, Hereford	**Gauge**: 7¼ inches, 5 inches, 3½ inches
Length of Line: 1 kilometre	**Web site**: www.hsme.co.uk

GENERAL INFORMATION

Nearest Mainline Station: Hereford (1½ miles)
Nearest Bus Station: Hereford (1½ miles)
Car Parking: Free parking available on site
Coach Parking: Available by prior arrangement
Souvenir Shop(s): Yes
Food & Drinks: Available

SPECIAL INFORMATION

The Broomy Hill Railway is operated by the
Hereford Society of Model Engineers and has two
separate tracks which run along the bank of the
River Wye. Entry to the site is free of charge and
picnic areas are available.

OPERATING INFORMATION

Opening Times: The second and last Sundays of
the month from Easter until September/October.
Trains run from 12.00pm to 5.00pm.
Steam Working: All operating days.
Prices: Adults £1.00 per ride
Children £1.00 per ride
Note: Six rides can be bought for £5.00

Detailed Directions by Car:
From the centre of Hereford, take the A49 Ross-on-Wye Road, turning right into Barton Road. After approximately
400 metres, turn left into Broomy Hill Road, proceed for around 600 metres before turning left following signs
for the Waterworks Museum. The railway is on the right just after the museum which is signposted with Brown
Tourist Information Signs.

BURNLEY & PENDLE MINIATURE RAILWAY

Contact Address: c/o Mr D. Kitson,
11 Deerstone Road, Nelson, Lancashire,
BB9 9LN
Telephone Nº: None
Year Formed: 1992
Location: Thompson Park, Burnley
Length of Line: ½ mile

Nº of Steam Locos: 4
Nº of Other Locos: 7
Nº of Members: 33
Annual Membership Fee: £10.00 Adults,
£6.00 Concessions, Students & Children
Approx Nº of Visitors P.A.: 6,000 – 9,000
Gauge: 7¼ inches
Web site: www.bpmrs.org.uk

GENERAL INFORMATION

Nearest Mainline Station: Burnley Central (1 mile)
Nearest Bus Station: Burnley (1 mile)
Car Parking: Available adjacent to Thompson Park
Coach Parking: Not available
Food & Drinks: Available from a kiosk in the Park

OPERATING INFORMATION

Opening Times: Sundays from Easter until the end of September. Trains run between 11.00am and 4.00pm.
Steam Working: Most operating days.
Prices: 50p per person per ride

Detailed Directions by Car:
The Railway runs through Thompson Park in Burnley. The main entrance to this is in Ormerod Road which is just a short distance from the town centre and also near to Turf Moor, the home of Burnley FC.

CANTERBURY & DISTRICT M.E.S.

Address: Brett Quarry, Fordwich, Near Canterbury, Kent
Phone Nº: (01227) 273357 (Secretary)
Year Formed: –
Location of Line: Brett Quarry, Fordwich
Length of Line: 750 feet

Nº of Steam Locos: (As provided by the
Nº of Other Locos: MES members)
Nº of Members: Approximately 60
Gauge: 3½ inches and 5 inches
Web site: www.cdmes.org.uk

GENERAL INFORMATION

Nearest Mainline Station: Sturry (½ mile)
Nearest Bus Station: Canterbury (3 miles)
Car Parking: None on site
Coach Parking: None
Food & Drinks: None

SPECIAL INFORMATION

The Canterbury & District Model Engineering Society runs a track on land kindly loaned by Bretts of Fordwich which is open to the public on some Sunday afternoons throughout the year, weather permitting.

OPERATING INFORMATION

Opening Times: 2007 dates: 8th April, 13th May, 10th June, 17th June, 8th July, 12th August, 9th September and 14th October. Trains run from 2.00pm to 5.00pm, weather permitting.
Steam Working: Most operating days depending on which locos have been provided by the MES members.
Prices: Free rides although donations are accepted for the upkeep of the track.

Detailed Directions by Car:
From the A28 at Sturry turn into Fordwich Road then left into Marlowe Meadows (look for the Brett sign). Drive towards the large green gates then walk through following the access road. Please note that the railway is on private land and access to the public is limited so please do not drive down this road as there is no parking on-site.

CANVEY MINIATURE RAILWAY

Address: Waterside Farm Sports Centre, Somnes Avenue, Canvey Island, Essex, SS8 9RA
Telephone Nº: (01268) 681679
Year Formed: 1997
Location of Line: Canvey Island
Length of Line: Two lines, one of 1,440 feet and one of 4,400 feet (7¼ inch line)

Nº of Steam Locos: Variable
Nº of Other Locos: Variable
Nº of Members: Approximately 100
Approx Nº of Visitors P.A.: 6,000
Gauge: 3½ inches, 5 inches & 7¼ inches
Web site: www.cramec.org

GENERAL INFORMATION

Nearest Mainline Station: Benfleet (1 mile)
Nearest Bus Station: Bus stop just outside
Car Parking: Available on site
Coach Parking: Available on site
Food & Drinks: None

SPECIAL INFORMATION

The railway is operated by members of the Canvey Railway and Model Engineering Club.

OPERATING INFORMATION

Opening Times: Every Sunday from the first Sunday in April until the second Sunday in October. Trains run from 10.30am to 4.00pm.
Steam Working: When available on operating days.
Prices: £1.00 per ride.
Also £5.00 for 6 rides or £9.00 for 12 rides.

Detailed Directions by Car:
All road routes to Canvey Island meet at the Waterside Farm roundabout. The railway lines are located in the grounds of the Sports Complex/Leisure Centre. Turn right at the traffic lights into the centre and the car park is on the left with the railway on the right.

CARDIFF MODEL ENGINEERING SOCIETY

Address: Heath Park, King George V Drive, Cardiff
Telephone Nº: None
Year Formed: 1948
Location of Line: Heath Park, Cardiff
Length of Line: 2 tracks of 1,000 feet each plus a tram track of 700 feet

Nº of Steam Locos: 8
Nº of Other Locos: 4
Nº of Members: Approximately 150
Approx Nº of Visitors P.A.: 7,000
Gauge: 3½ inches, 5 inches & 7¼ inches
Web site: www.cardiffmes.com

GENERAL INFORMATION

Nearest Mainline Station: Heath Low Level (½ mile)
Nearest Bus Station: Cardiff
Car Parking: Available on site and also nearby
Coach Parking: None
Food & Drinks: Available

SPECIAL INFORMATION

The Cardiff Model Engineering society moved to Heath Park in 1987. The site, which includes two railway tracks and a unique electric tramway, two model railways, and extensive refreshment facilities, has been developed by the members for the benefit of visitors.

OPERATING INFORMATION

Opening Times: 2007 public dates: 25th March; 8th & 9th April; 6th, 27th & 28th May; 24th June; 29th July; 26th & 27th August; 23rd September; 14th October. Trains run from 1.00pm to 5.00pm.
Steam Working: All operating days.
Prices: £1.00 entry per person then £1.00 per ride.

Detailed Directions by Car:
Exit the M4 at Junction 32 and travel towards Cardiff. Turn left at the 3rd set of traffic lights (by the Tesco garage) and continue through 3 sets of traffic lights to the T-junction lights. Turn left here then immediately right then take the 1st left onto King George V Drive. Turn left at the roundabout and take the lane 400 yards on the right.

CELYN WOOD RAILWAY

Address: Northop Garden Centre, Northop, Mold, Flintshire CH7 6AA **Phone Nº**: (01352) 750492 (Secretary) **Year Formed**: 1975 **Location of Line**: In the grounds of the Welsh College of Horticulture **Length of Line**: 1,700 feet	**Nº of Steam Locos**: 42 **Nº of Other Locos**: 8 **Nº of Members**: Approximately 70 **Approx Nº of Visitors P.A.**: 6,000 **Gauge**: 3½ inches and 5 inches **Web site**: www.moldmes.com

GENERAL INFORMATION

Nearest Mainline Station: Chester (12 miles)
Nearest Bus Station: Mold (3 miles)
Car Parking: Available on site
Coach Parking: Available by prior arrangement
Food & Drinks: None

SPECIAL INFORMATION

The Celyn Wood Railway is operated by members of the Mold Model Engineering Society. The track runs through the Northop Garden Centre in the grounds of the Welsh College of Horticulture.

OPERATING INFORMATION

Opening Times: Sundays throughout the year weather and available staff permitting. Trains run from 11.00am to 4.00pm.
Steam Working: Most Sundays.
Prices: 50p per person per ride although prices may vary during Special events.

Detailed Directions by Car:
The Welsh College of Horticulture is signposted from the crossroads where the A5119 meets the B5126 at traffic lights in the village of Northop. From Mold: Take the A5119 towards Flint and turn left at the traffic lights once in Northop; From the West: Take the A55 towards Chester, turn right onto the A5119 and turn right at the traffic lights in Northop. The College is approximately ¼ mile from the lights. Turn right into the Garden Centre entrance and follow the train signs.

CHELMSFORD SOCIETY MODEL ENGINEERS

Address: Meteor Way (off Waterhouse Lane), Chelmsford, Essex
Telephone N°: None
Year Formed: 1935
Location of Line: Chelmsford
Length of Line: Two tracks, each approximately 1,000 feet long

N° of Steam Locos: 40+ (owned by
N° of Other Locos: 10+ members)
N° of Members: Approximately 75
Approx N° of Visitors P.A.: 1,500
Gauge: 3½ inches, 5 inches & 7¼ inches
Web site:
www.chelmsford-miniature-railway.org.uk

GENERAL INFORMATION

Nearest Mainline Station: Chelmsford (½ mile)
Nearest Bus Station: Chelmsford (½ mile)
Car Parking: Available adjacent to the railway (currently free of charge at weekends)
Food & Drinks: Light refreshments available

SPECIAL INFORMATION

The Chelmsford Society of Model Engineers promotes the safe construction and operation of passenger-carrying steam, electric and diesel hauled trains, traction engines and other scale models.

OPERATING INFORMATION

Opening Times: Every Sunday from May to 23rd September inclusive. Also Santa Specials on 2nd December 2007. Trains run from 2.00pm to 5.00pm. Please check the Society's web site for further details.
Steam Working: Most operating days.
Prices: 50p per person per ride. 12 rides are available for the price of £5.00

Detailed Directions by Car:
From London: Follow the A12 then take the A1016 towards Chelmsford town centre. Continue past the A414 junctions into Westway then into Waterhouse Lane. Meteor Way is on the right after the fourth set of traffic lights, just before the river. Park and then proceed past the five bar gate to the club entrance on the right; From Southend: Follow the A130 to the A12 junction then cross onto the A1114. After 1¼ miles join the A414 towards Chelmsford. Follow the A414 around Chelmsford to the junction with the A1016 at Widford. Take the 2nd exit into Westway then as from London; From Colchester: Follow the A12 and exit at the A414 junction towards Chelmsford. Follow the A414 to the A1016, then as from Southend.

CHESTERFIELD & DISTRICT M.E.S.

Address: The Clubhouse, Hady Hill, Bolsover Road, Chesterfield S41 0EE
Telephone Nº: None
Year Formed: 1932
Location of Line: In the grounds of St. Peter & St. Paul School, Chesterfield
Length of Line: Two lines – one of 1,100 feet and one of 2,000 feet

Nº of Steam Locos: 1 + members engines
Nº of Other Locos: 1 + members engines
Nº of Members: Approximately 210
Annual Membership Fee: £25.00 (Adult)
Approx Nº of Visitors P.A.: 5,000
Gauge: 2½ inches, 3½ inches, 5 inches and 7¼ inches
Web site: www.cdmes.co.uk

GENERAL INFORMATION

Nearest Mainline Station: Chesterfield (1½ miles)
Nearest Bus Station: Chesterfield (1 mile)
Car Parking: Available on site
Coach Parking: Available by prior arrangement
Food & Drinks: Available

SPECIAL INFORMATION

The Society's aims are to bring together persons from all walks of life who share a common interest in miniature engineering in all its forms.
The excellent facilities at Hady include tracks for locomotives and there are also areas for traction engines to show their paces. As the land is undulating, both the ground level and raised tracks make challenging driving for all locomotives.

OPERATING INFORMATION

Opening Times: Usually the third Saturday of the month throughout the year plus some other open days. Trains run from 12.30pm to 4.30pm. Please contact the railway for further details.
Steam Working: All operational days.
Prices: Admission is free. Rides are 50p per person per ride.

Detailed Directions by Car:
The Society is located on the top of Hady Hill, two-thirds of a mile from the town on Bolsover Road, A632. Driving out of Chesterfield, as you get to the top of the steep hill, turn left off the main road into the grounds of St. Peter & St. Paul School. Follow the drive around to the left and then take the first right. The site is at the end of the drive, after about 250 yards.

CHINGFORD & DISTRICT M.E.C.

Address: Ridgeway Park, Peel Close, Old Church Road, Chingford   E4
Telephone N°: None
Year Formed: 1945
Location: Ridgeway Park, Chingford
Length of Lines: 1,000 feet (5 inch line) and 3,000 feet (7¼ inch line)

N° of Steam Locos: 11 (owned by Club)
N° of Other Locos: Many
N° of Members: Approximately 90
Annual Membership Fee: £25.00 Adult
Approx N° of Visitors P.A.: 17,000
Gauge: 3½ inches, 5 inches & 7¼ inches
Web site: www.cadmec.co.uk

GENERAL INFORMATION

Nearest Mainline Station: Chingford (1½ miles)
Nearest Underground Station: Walthamstow Central (5 miles)
Car Parking: Limited spaces within the Park
Coach Parking: None
Food & Drinks: None

SPECIAL INFORMATION

The Chingford & District Model Engineering Club seeks to promote all forms of model engineering and model making. It's members come from all walks of life, and do not necessarily have an engineering background.

OPERATING INFORMATION

Opening Times: Sundays and Bank Holidays from April to September inclusive. Train rides usually start at 2.00pm.
Steam Working: Practically every operating day.
Prices: 40p per person per ride on the raised track
70p per person per ride on the ground track

Detailed Directions by Car:
Ridgeway Park is situated off the A112 Old Church Road in Chingford. Turn into Peel Close and the Park entrance is on the left after 50 yards at the mini-roundabout. A small car park is situated in Ridgeway Park. The railway itself is located about 150 yards down the main path on the right.

COALYARD MINIATURE RAILWAY

Address: c/o Severn Valley Railway, Comberton Road, Kidderminster, DY10 1QX **Telephone Nº:** (0121) 552-5148 **Year Formed:** 1988 **Location of Line:** Kidderminster Town Station at the Severn Valley Railway	**Length of Line:** 450 yards **Nº of Steam Locos:** 2 (+ visiting locos) **Nº of Other Locos:** 2 (+ visiting locos) **Nº of Members:** Approximately 12 **Approx Nº of Visitors P.A.:** 60,000 **Gauge:** 7¼ inches

GENERAL INFORMATION

Nearest Mainline Station: Kidderminster (adjacent)
Nearest Bus Station: Kidderminster (¼ mile)
Car Parking: Pay & Display car park is adjacent
Coach Parking: Available
Souvenir Shop(s): Severn Valley Railway Shop is adjacent
Food & Drinks: Available from the adjacent Kidderminster Museum and Severn Valley Railway Restaurant.

SPECIAL INFORMATION

The Coalyard Miniature Railway is based at the Severn Valley Railway's Kidderminster Town Station and raises funds for the Station and other projects on the Severn Valley Railway.

OPERATING INFORMATION

Opening Times: Most Saturdays, Sundays and Bank Holidays throughout the year. Please contact the railway for further information.
Steam Working: On selected dates only. Please contact the railway for further details.
Prices: 70p per person per ride.

Detailed Directions by Car:
Exit the M5 at Junction 3 and follow the brown tourist signs for the Severn Valley Railway. Alternatively exit the M42 at Junction 1 orthe M5 at Junction 4 and take the A448 from Bromsgrove to Kidderminster before once again following the brown tourist signs for the Severn Valley Railway.

COATE WATER PARK MINIATURE RAILWAY

Address: Coate Water Country Park,
Swindon, Wiltshire
Telephone Nº: None
Year Formed: 1964
Location of Line: Coate Water Country
Park, Swindon
Length of Line: ½ mile

Nº of Steam/Other Locos: A number of
different locos are supplied for use by
members of the Society
Nº of Members: Approximately 60
Approx Nº of Visitors P.A.: Not known
Gauge: 5 inches and 7¼ inches

GENERAL INFORMATION

Nearest Mainline Station: Swindon (2 miles)
Nearest Bus Station: Swindon (2 miles)
Car Parking: Available in the Park
Coach Parking: None
Food & Drinks: None

SPECIAL INFORMATION

The Coate Water Park Miniature Railway is operated
by volunteers from the North Wiltshire Model
Engineering Society.

OPERATING INFORMATION

Opening Times: Sunday afternoons (weather
permitting). Open from 11.00am with trains
running until approximately 5.00pm.
Steam Working: Depends which locos have been
provided for use on the day by the individual
members.
Prices: 50p per person per ride.

Detailed Directions by Car:
From Junction 15 of the M4, take the A419 towards Swindon to the first roundabout (Common Head). Take the
first exit at this roundabout along Marlborough Road past the Great Western Hospital. Take the left turn just
before the 40 mph sign then the first turn on the right leads directly to the railway site.

CONWY VALLEY RAILWAY MUSEUM

Address: Old Goods Yard, Betws-y-Coed, Conwy, North Wales LL24 0AL	**Nº of Steam Locos**: 4
	Nº of Other Locos: 2
Telephone Nº: (01690) 710568	**Nº of Members**: –
Year Formed: 1983	**Annual Membership Fee**: –
Location of Line: Betws-y-Coed	**Approx Nº of Visitors P.A.**: 50,000
Length of Line: One and an eighth miles	**Gauge**: 7¼ inches and 15 inches
	Web site: www.conwyrailwaymuseum.co.uk

GENERAL INFORMATION

Nearest Mainline Station: Betws-y-Coed (20 yards)
Nearest Bus Station: 40 yards
Car Parking: Car park at site
Coach Parking: Car park at site
Souvenir Shop(s): Yes
Food & Drinks: Yes – Buffet Coach Cafe

SPECIAL INFORMATION

The Museum houses the unique 3D dioramas by the late Jack Nelson. Also the ¼ size steam loco 'Britannia'. The Railway now has two Isle of Man locos – "Douglas" and "Dragonfly" and a Tinkerbell loco "Petunia" is currently on loan.

OPERATING INFORMATION

Opening Times: Daily from 10.00am to 5.30pm.
Trains Working: Daily from 10.15am
Prices: Adult – £1.50 museum entry;
Train rides £1.50; Tram rides £1.00
Child/Senior Citizen – £1.00 museum entry;
Train rides £1.50; Tram rides £1.00
Family tickets – £4.00

Detailed Directions by Car:
From Midlands & South: Take M54/M6 onto the A5 and into Betws-y-Coed; From Other Parts: Take the A55 coast road then the A470 to Betws-y-Coed. The museum is located by the Mainline Station directly off the A5.

CROWBOROUGH LOCOMOTIVE SOCIETY

Address: Goldsmiths Leisure Centre, Eridge Road, Crowborough   TN6 2TN
Telephone Nº: (01892) 852741
Year Formed: 1990
Location of Line: Crowborough
Length of Line: ¼ mile circuit

Nº of Steam Locos: 10
Nº of Other Locos: 8
Nº of Members: 27 at present
Approx Nº of Visitors P.A.: 900
Gauge: 3½ inches and 5 inches
Web site: www.geocities.com/crolocsoc/

GENERAL INFORMATION

Nearest Mainline Station: Crowborough (1½ miles)
Nearest Bus Station: Tunbridge Wells (7 miles)
Car Parking: Available on site
Coach Parking: Available on site
Food & Drinks: Available at the Leisure Centre

SPECIAL INFORMATION

The Crowborough Locomotive Society was formed to build, maintain, and run a miniature railway at the Goldsmiths Leisure Centre in Crowborough. The society runs live steam working locomotives to give both young and old alike a railway journey in miniature!

OPERATING INFORMATION

Opening Times: Saturday afternoons and selected Sundays from Easter until the end of October. Trains run from 2.30pm to 4.45pm.
Steam Working: Most operational days.
Prices: £1.00 per person for two circuits of the track.

Detailed Directions by Car:
Goldsmiths Leisure Centre is situated in the north of Crowborough just off the A26 (Eridge Road) which is the main Tunbridge Wells to Uckfield through road.

CUTTESLOWE PARK MINIATURE RAILWAY

Address: Cutteslowe Park, Harbord Road, Oxford   OX2 8ES
Phone Nº: (01235) 770836 (Secretary)
Year Formed: 1955
Location: Cutteslowe Park, Oxford
Length of Line: Two lines – 390 yard raised line and 250 yard ground level line

Nº of Steam Locos: 40
Nº of Other Locos: 10
Nº of Members: Approximately 110
Approx Nº of Visitors P.A.: 10,000
Gauge: 3½ inches, 5 inches & 7¼ inches
Web site: www.cosme.org.uk

GENERAL INFORMATION

Nearest Mainline Station: Oxford (3¼ miles)
Nearest Bus Station: Oxford (3 miles)
Car Parking: Available on site
Coach Parking: Available by prior arrangement
Food & Drinks: Refreshments are available in Cutteslowe Park

SPECIAL INFORMATION

The Cutteslowe Park Miniature Railway is operated by the City of Oxford Society of Model Engineers.

OPERATING INFORMATION

Opening Times: The railway opens on the 1st, 3rd and 5th Sundays each month as well as Bank Holidays from April to October. Trains run from 2.00pm to 5.30pm (4.30pm in October). Trains also run on Wednesdays in August – 1.00pm to 4.30pm.
Steam Working: Up to 5 steam locomotives run on every operating day.
Prices: Adults 60p
Children 60p
10 rides are available for £5.50

Detailed Directions by Car:
From outside of Oxford join the ringroad and head to the North of the city. At the roundabout at the junction of the A40 ringroad and the A4165 Banbury Road, head North signposted for Kidlington. Take the third turn on the right into Harbord Road which leads directly into the Park. Follow the signs from the car park for the Railway.

DEVON RAILWAY CENTRE

Address: Bickleigh, Tiverton, Devon, EX16 8RG
Telephone Nº: (01884) 855671
Year Formed: 1997
Location of Line: Bickleigh, Devon
Length of Line: ½ mile (7¼ inch and 2 foot gauges); 200 yards (Standard gauge)

Nº of Steam Locos: 3
Nº of Other Locos: 15
Nº of Members: None
Approx Nº of Visitors P.A.: –
Gauge: 7¼ inches, 2 feet and Standard
Web site: www.devonrailwaycentre.co.uk

GENERAL INFORMATION

Nearest Mainline Station: Exeter
Nearest Bus Station: Tiverton (Route 55)
Car Parking: Available on site
Coach Parking: Available on site
Souvenir Shop(s): Yes
Food & Drinks: Yes

SPECIAL INFORMATION

Devon Railway Centre has passenger carrying lines and also features a large model railway exhibition with 15 working layouts. New for 2007 is an Edwardian model village built to a 1:12 scale.

OPERATING INFORMATION

Opening Times: Daily 6th–22nd April then 23rd May to 9th September & 20th–28th October. Closed Mondays during June. Open Wednesday to Friday & Weekends from 9th–20th May and 12th to 30th September. Open during Weekends in October and May Bank Holiday weekend. Open from 10.30am until 5.00pm on each of these days.
Steam Working: Trains may be steam or diesel hauled so please phone for further information.
Prices: Adult £5.60   Child £4.60
          Senior Citizen £4.80   Family £17.30
Admission includes unlimited train rides and access to the model village, model railways and museum.

Detailed Directions by Car:
From All Parts: Devon Railway Centre is situated adjacent to the famous Bickleigh Bridge, just off the A396 Exeter to Tiverton road (3 miles from Tiverton and 8 miles from Exeter).

DOCKLAND & EAST LONDON M.E.S.

Address: Belhus Woods Country Park, Romford Road, Aveley, Essex
Phone Nº: (01708) 228510 (Secretary)
Year Formed: 1985
Location: Belhus Woods Country park
Length of Line: 500 feet

Nº of Steam Locos: 3
Nº of Other Locos: 3
Nº of Members: 32
Approx Nº of Visitors P.A.: 400
Gauge: 5 inches and 7¼ inches

GENERAL INFORMATION

Nearest Mainline Station: Upminster (4 miles)
Nearest Bus Station: Grays (5 miles). Arriva bus service 373 will stop at Belhus Woods and collect passengers there on request although there is no stop.
Car Parking: Pay & Display parking available on site
Coach Parking: Available by prior arrangement
Souvenir Shop(s): Yes – Country Park shop
Food & Drinks: Light refreshments available

SPECIAL INFORMATION

The Railway is located in Belhus Woods which is a beautiful Country Park which has barbecue areas adjacent to the track and woodland walks through areas full of waterfowl.

OPERATING INFORMATION

Opening Times: During the first weekend of every month from April to October inclusive. Trains run from 12.00pm to 4.30pm.
Steam Working: Both Steam-hauled and Electric services run on every operating day.
Prices: 50p per person per ride.

Detailed Directions by Car:
Exit the M25 at Junction 29 and follow the A127 towards Romford. After 1 mile turn off at the Hall Lane exit by the flyover and head South towards Upminster. Continue down Hall Lane following through into Station Road then Corbets Tey Road. Upon reaching the T-junction turn right into Harwood Hall Lane then left at the mini-roundabout into Aveley Road. Belhus Woods Country Park is on the left after about 1¼ miles.

DUNHAM'S WOOD LIGHT RAILWAY

Address: Dunham's Wood, Rodham
Road, March   PE15 0DN
Phone Nº: (01760) 338052 (Chairman)
Year Formed: 1989
Location of Line: Just off the B1099 in
March, Cambridgeshire
Length of Line: Approximately ½ mile

Nº of Steam Locos: 0
Nº of Other Locos: 8
Nº of Members: Approximately 20
Approx Nº of Visitors P.A.: 1,200
Gauge: 7¼ inches
Web site: www.dunhamswood.co.uk

GENERAL INFORMATION

Nearest Mainline Station: March (3 miles)
Nearest Bus Station: March (2 miles)
Car Parking: Available on site
Coach Parking: Available on site
Food & Drinks: Available on open days

OPERATING INFORMATION

Opening Times: Easter Sunday & Monday, May
Bank Holiday Sunday & Monday, Whitsun Sunday &
Monday, the last Sunday in July, every Sunday and
Bank Holiday in August. Trains run from 2.00pm to
5.00pm.
Steam Working: Only when steam locos visit.
Prices: Adults £1.00
            Children 50p
Note: An extra fee is also charged for entrance to
the Wood.

Detailed Directions by Car:
From the A141 North or South, follow directions to March town centre. From here follow the B1099 signposted
for Christchurch. After 1 mile cross the railway line then take the next turning on the left into Binnimoor Road.
After 1 mile turn right into Rodham Road and the wood is on the left after 200 metres with the Car Park opposite.

EASTBOURNE MINIATURE STEAM RAILWAY

Address: Lottbridge Drove, Eastbourne, East Sussex BN23 6NS
Telephone Nº: (01323) 520229
Year Formed: 1992
Location of Line: Eastbourne
Length of Line: 1 mile

Nº of Steam Locos: 6
Nº of Other Locos: 3
Nº of Members: –
Approx Nº of Visitors P.A.: –
Gauge: 7¼ inches
Web site: www.emsr.co.uk

GENERAL INFORMATION

Nearest Mainline Station: Eastbourne (2 miles)
Nearest Bus Station: Eastbourne (2 miles)
Car Parking: Free parking on site
Coach Parking: Free parking on site
Souvenir Shop(s): Yes
Food & Drinks: Yes

SPECIAL INFORMATION

The Railway site also has many other attractions including model railways, an adventure playground, nature walk, maze, picnic area and a Cafe.

OPERATING INFORMATION

Opening Times: Open 10.00am to 5.00pm daily from 31st March until 30th September. Also special events on Easter Sunday.
Steam Working: Weekends, Bank Holidays and during School Holidays. Diesel at other times.
Prices: Adult £4.45
　　　　　 Child £3.95 (2 years and under free)
　　　　　 Family Tickets £16.00
　　　　　　　　　　　 (2 adults + 2 children)

Detailed Directions by Car:
From All Parts: Take the A22 new road to Eastbourne then follow the Brown tourist signs for the 'Mini Railway'.

EAST HERTS MINIATURE RAILWAY

Address: Van Hage Garden Centre, Great Amwell, near Ware SG12 9RP	**Nº of Steam Locos**: 3
Telephone Nº: (020) 8292-2997	**Nº of Other Locos**: 2
Year Formed: 1978	**Nº of Members**: Approximately 40
Location: Van Hage Garden Centre	**Annual Membership Fee**: £12.00
Length of Line: 500 metres	**Approx Nº of Visitors P.A.**: 40,000
	Gauge: 7¼ inches
	Web site: www.ehmr.org.uk

GENERAL INFORMATION

Nearest Mainline Station: Ware (1½ miles)
Nearest Bus Station: Bus stop outside the Centre
Car Parking: Available on site
Coach Parking: Available
Food & Drinks: Available in the Garden Centre

SPECIAL INFORMATION

The Railway operates a line at the Van Hage Garden Centre in Great Amwell. The railway is run by volunteers and any profits are donated to the local special needs school and other local charities.

OPERATING INFORMATION

Opening Times: Weekends and Bank Holidays throughout the year. Also open daily during the school holidays.
Steam Working: Most operating days.
Prices: 70p per person per ride. Under-2s travel free of charge.

Detailed Directions by Car:
From the South: Take the A10 towards Cambridge and exit at the first Ware junction signposted for A414. Take the 2nd exit at the roundabout onto the A1170 towards Ware and Van Hage Garden Centre is on the left after 600 metres; From the East: Take the A414 from Harlow and turn off onto the A1170 for Ware. Then as above.

ESK VALLEY MODEL ENGINEERING SOCIETY

Contact Address: c/o Lady Victoria Colliery, Newtongrange, Midlothian
Phone Nº: (0131) 660-3898 (Secretary)
Year Formed: 1982
Location of Line: Vogrie Country Park
Length of Line: 2000 feet

Nº of Steam Locos: 5 (Member's locos)
Nº of Other Locos: 5
Nº of Members: 26
Approx Nº of Visitors P.A.: 4,000+
Gauge: 3½ inches, 5 inches & 7¼ inches

GENERAL INFORMATION

Nearest Mainline Station: Edinburgh (9 miles)
Nearest Bus Station: Dalkeith (3 miles)
Car Parking: Available on site
Coach Parking: Available on site
Food & Drinks: Available

SPECIAL INFORMATION

The Esk Valley MES operates a railway in the grounds of the Vogrie Country Park which comprises 105 hectares of woods and Victorian parkland including a 1876 Victorian mansion (part of which is open to the public), a nine-hole golf course, adventure playground and a cafeteria.

OPERATING INFORMATION

Opening Times: Sundays from Easter to September. Trains run from 2.00pm to 5.00pm.
Steam Working: Most operating days.
Prices: £1.00 per person per ride.

Detailed Directions by Car:
From Dalkeith: Travel South on the A68 for 2½ miles then turn right onto the B6372 signposted for Vogrie Country Park. Continue along this road for the Park; From the A7: Travel towards Gorbridge and turn off onto the B6372. Pass through Gorbridge staying on the B6372, continue through Newlandrig for the Park.

EVERGREENS MINIATURE RAILWAY

Address: Main Road, Stickney, Boston, Lincolnshire
Telephone Nº: (01406) 701612
Year Formed: 2002
Location of Line: Stickney, off the A16
Length of Line: 500 metres of 7¼ inch gauge and 280 metres of 5 inch gauge

Nº of Steam Locos: 20
Nº of Other Locos: 15
Nº of Members: Approximately 20
Approx Nº of Visitors P.A.: Not known
Gauge: 5 inches and 7¼ inches
Web site: www.evergreensrail.co.uk

GENERAL INFORMATION

Nearest Mainline Station: Boston (10 miles)
Nearest Bus Station: Boston (10 miles)
Car Parking: Available on site
Coach Parking: None
Food & Drinks: Available

SPECIAL INFORMATION

The site of the railway was previously a Horticultural Nursery and is around 3 acres in size. The site currently has 3 level crossings, 3 bridges and 2 ponds and is always undergoing expansion.

OPERATING INFORMATION

Opening Times: The last Saturday of each month from April to October. Trains run from 10.00am to 4.00pm.
Steam Working: Most operating days.
Prices: No charge for rides but donations for further development of the line are accepted.

Detailed Directions by Car:
The railway is situated on the A16 between Boston and Spilsby. Upon reaching the village of Stickney, look out for the signal on the grass verge which marks the entrance to the railway.

FANCOTT MINIATURE RAILWAY

Address: Fancott Miniature Railway, Fancott, near Toddington, Bedfordshire
Telephone Nº: (01525) 872366
Year Formed: 1996
Location of Line: The Fancott Pub, near Toddington, Bedfordshire
Length of Line: ¼ mile

Nº of Steam Locos: 0
Nº of Other Locos: 3
Nº of Members: 8
Annual Membership Fee: £30.00
Approx Nº of Visitors P.A.: 10,000
Gauge: 7¼ inches
Web site: www.thefancott.co.uk

GENERAL INFORMATION

Nearest Mainline Station: Harlington/Leagrave
Nearest Bus Station: Luton
Car Parking: 50 spaces available on site
Coach Parking: Available but no special space
Souvenir Shop(s): No
Food & Drinks: Pub/Restaurant on site

SPECIAL INFORMATION

The Railway runs through the grounds of The Fancott Pub, winner of the Whitbread Family Pub of the Year in 2000.

OPERATING INFORMATION

Opening Times: Open between Mothers Day and 31st September. 1.00pm to 5.00pm Monday to Thursday, 1.00pm to dusk Friday and Saturday and 12.00pm to 6.00pm on Sundays and Bank Holidays. Only open on weekdays during the School Holidays however.
Steam Working: Steam locos visit on a regular basis – see the website for details.
Prices: £1.00 Adults and Children

Detailed Directions by Car:
From All Parts: Exit the M1 at Junction 12 and travel towards Toddington. After approximately 100 yards, take the B579 towards Chalton and Fancott. The Fancott pub is on the left after the second bend.

FENLAND LIGHT RAILWAY

Address: Mereside Farm, Mereside Drove, Ramsey Mereside, Cambs.
Telephone Nº: None
Year Formed: 1991
Location of Line: Mereside Farm
Length of Line: 800 feet

Nº of Steam Locos: 3+
Nº of Other Locos: 2+
Nº of Members: 12
Approx Nº of Visitors P.A.: 500 – 1,000
Gauge: 7¼ inches

GENERAL INFORMATION

Nearest Mainline Station: Peterborough (10 miles)
Nearest Bus Station: Peterborough (10 miles)
Car Parking: Available on site
Coach Parking: None
Food & Drinks: Available

SPECIAL INFORMATION

The railway is operated by volunteers from the Ramsey Miniature Steam Railway Society.

OPERATING INFORMATION

Opening Times: The third Sunday of each month from April to October inclusive except for August when two days are spent at the nearby RAF Upwood fair. There are also two Santa Special running days near to the Christmas holidays and at least two other charity running days when proceeds go to a local charity.
Steam Working: All operating days.
Prices: £1.00 per ride

Detailed Directions by Car:
From Ramsey: Travel up Great Whyte, turn right at the mini-roundabout by the Mill Apartments and follow onto Stocking Fen Road. Follow this road for just over a mile then turn left into Bodsey Toll Road for Ramsey Mereside. Follow this road until the signpost for Ramsey Mereside and turn right into Mereside Drove. The railway is on the left after approximately 1 mile.

FRIMLEY LODGE MINIATURE RAILWAY

Address: Frimley Lodge Park, Sturt Road, Frimley Green, Surrey
Phone Nº: 07710 606461 (Please use on operating days only)
Year Formed: 1991
Location of Line: Frimley Green
Length of Line: 1 kilometre

Nº of Steam Locos: 5 (Members' locos)
Nº of Other Locos: 3
Nº of Members: Approximately 60
Approx Nº of Visitors P.A.: 20,000+
Gauge: 3½ inches, 5 inches & 7¼ inches
Web site: www.flmr.org

GENERAL INFORMATION

Nearest Mainline Station: Frimley (2 miles)
Nearest Bus Station: Farnborough (4 miles) – No buses on a Sunday however!
Car Parking: Available on site
Coach Parking: Available by prior arrangement
Food & Drinks: Cafe in the Park

SPECIAL INFORMATION

The Railway is operated by volunteers from the Frimley and Ascot Locomotive Club who bring their own Locomotives, some from as far away as Crewkerne, to give pleasure to others. All the proceeds are used for the maintenance of the Railway and to benefit local charities.

OPERATING INFORMATION

Opening Times: The first Sunday of the month from March to November. Also on August Bank Holiday and Wednesdays during the school holidays (subject to staff availability). Trains run from 11.00am to 5.00pm on Sundays and from 11.00am – 1.00pm then 2.00pm – 4.00pm when open on Wednesdays.
Steam Working: Operational Sundays only.
Prices: 80p for single rides or £1.20 for double rides.

Detailed Directions by Car:
Exit the M3 at Junction 4 and take the A331 towards Guildford. Leave the A331 at the turn-off for Mytchett and turn left at the top of the ramp then left again at the Miners Arms into Sturt Road. Cross over the bridge then turn right into Frimley Lodge Park. Once in the Park turn right then right again then take the next left for the Railway.

GOFFS PARK LIGHT RAILWAY

Correspondence: c/o 8 Le May Close, Horley, Surrey RH6 7JH	**N° of Steam Locos**: 15
Telephone N°: None	**N° of Other Locos**: 6
Year Formed: 1958	**N° of Members**: Approximately 30
Location of Line: Goffs Park, Crawley	**Approx N° of Visitors P.A.**: 5,000
Length of Line: 1,200 feet	**Gauge**: 3½ inches and 5 inches

GENERAL INFORMATION

Nearest Mainline Station: Crawley (½ mile)
Nearest Bus Station: Crawley (½ mile)
Car Parking: Limited parking available on site
Coach Parking: None
Food & Drinks: None

OPERATING INFORMATION

Opening Times: Sundays and Bank Holidays from Easter to October. Trains run from 2.00pm to 5.00pm.
Steam Working: Most operating days.
Prices: 30p per ride.

Detailed Directions by Car:
Goffs Park is located near the centre of Crawley in Horsham Road (the A2220), adjacent to the level crossing with the mainline railway.

GOLDING SPRING MINIATURE RAILWAY

Address: Quainton Road Station, Quainton, Aylesbury, Bucks. HP22 4BY
Phone Nº: (01296) 623540 (Secretary)
Year Formed: 1972
Location: Within the Buckinghamshire Railway Centre site
Length of Line: 1,200 yards

Nº of Steam Locos: 12
Nº of Other Locos: 4
Nº of Members: Approximately 120
Approx Nº of Visitors P.A.: 25,000
Gauge: 3½ inches, 5 inches & 7¼ inches

GENERAL INFORMATION

Nearest Mainline Station: Aylesbury (6 miles)
Nearest Bus Station: Aylesbury (6 miles)
Car Parking: Free parking for 500 cars available
Coach Parking: Free parking for 10 coaches
Souvenir Shop(s): Yes
Food & Drinks: Yes

SPECIAL INFORMATION

The Golding Spring Miniature Railway is operated by members of the Vale of Aylesbury Model Engineering Society and is located at the Buckinghamshire Railway Centre.

OPERATING INFORMATION

Opening Times: Sundays and Bank Holidays from March to October inclusive. Also on Wednesdays in the school holidays to coincide with the Bucks Railway Centre. Trains run from 10.30am to 4.30pm
Steam Working: Every operational day.
Prices: 70p per ride
　　　　Under-3s travel free of charge

Detailed Directions by Car:
The Buckinghamshire Railway Centre is signposted off the A41 Aylesbury to Bicester Road at Waddesdon and off the A413 Buckingham to Aylesbury road at Whitchurch. Junctions 7, 8 and 9 of the M40 are all close by.

GREENHEAD PARK MINIATURE RAILWAY

Correspondence: 39 Lascelles Hall Road, Kirkheaton, Huddersfield	**Nº of Steam Locos**: 6
Telephone Nº: None	**Nº of Other Locos**: 4
Year Formed: 1944	**Nº of Members**: 46
Location: Greenhead Park, Huddersfield	**Approx Nº of Visitors P.A.**: 10,000
Length of Line: One third of a mile	**Gauge**: 5 inches and 7¼ inches
	Web site: www.hsme.me.uk

GENERAL INFORMATION

Nearest Mainline Station: Huddersfield (½ mile)
Nearest Bus Station: Huddersfield (½ mile)
Car Parking: Available on site
Coach Parking: Available on site
Food & Drinks: Available

SPECIAL INFORMATION

The Greenhead Park Miniature Railway is operated by members of the Huddersfield Society of Model Engineers. The Railway has a locomotive which is able to cater for passengers in wheelchairs.

OPERATING INFORMATION

Opening Times: Every Saturday and Sunday from March until Christmas Eve.
Steam Working: Every operating day.
Prices: £1.00 per person per ride or £2.50 for up to 5 people.

Detailed Directions by Car:
From the West: Exit the M62 at Junction 23 and follow the A640 New Hey Road towards the town centre. Continue along the A640 going straight on at two roundabouts then, after 500 yards, turn right into Park Drive for Greenhead Park; From the East: Exit the M62 at Junction 24 and take the A629 towards Huddersfield. At Ainley Top roundabout take the 4th exit onto A629 Halifax Road and after approximately 1½ miles turn right at the traffic signals into Edgerton Grove Road signposted for Marsh, Paddock and Lindley. Turn left at the roundabout onto A640 Trinity Street then right into Park Drive for Greenhead Park.

GRIMSBY & CLEETHORPES M.E.S.

Address: Waltham Windmill, Brigsley Road, Waltham, Grimsby
Telephone Nº: None
Year Formed: 1985
Location: Waltham, near Grimsby
Length of Line: 1,300 feet for 7¼ and 5 inch gauges, 600 feet for 3½ gauge

Nº of Steam Locos: 1
Nº of Other Locos: 1
Nº of Members: Approximately 80
Approx Nº of Visitors P.A.: Not known
Gauge: 3½ inches, 5 inches & 7¼ inches
Web site: www.gcmes.org.uk

GENERAL INFORMATION

Nearest Mainline Station: Grimsby (3 miles)
Nearest Bus Station: Grimsby (3 miles)
Car Parking: Available on site
Coach Parking: None
Food & Drinks: Available at the Windmill

SPECIAL INFORMATION

The Society's track is based in Waltham, near Grimsby adjacent to a preserved windmill dating back to 1878 which still operates from time to time.

OPERATING INFORMATION

Opening Times: Sundays and Bank Holidays from April to October inclusive. Trains run from 1.00pm to 4.00pm.
Steam Working: Most operating days.
Prices: 40p per ride.

Detailed Directions by Car:
The Railway is situated by Waltham Windmill on the B1203 Grimsby to Binbrook Road and is well signposted. The B1203 connects to the A16 at Scartho, a suburb of Grimsby, about a mile from the railway or to the A18 at Ashby Top, about 3 miles away.

HARLINGTON LOCOMOTIVE SOCIETY

Address: High Street, Harlington, Hayes, Middlesex UB3 5ET
Telephone Nº: None
Year Formed: 1947
Location of Line: Harlington High Street
Length of Line: 1,047 feet

Nº of Steam Locos: 40 (Members' locos)
Nº of Other Locos: Several
Nº of Members: Approximately 65
Approx Nº of Visitors P.A.: 3,000
Gauge: 3½ inches and 5 inches
Web site: www.harlingtonlocomotivesociety.org.uk

GENERAL INFORMATION

Nearest Mainline Station: Hayes (1½ miles)
Nearest Bus Stop: 50 yards – Services 90, H98 & 140
Car Parking: Limited on site parking. Also street parking available.
Coach Parking: None
Food & Drinks: Light refreshments are available

SPECIAL INFORMATION

Approximately 40 Steam plus several Electric locos are owned by individual members. Typically 4 locos will be in steam on most open days.

OPERATING INFORMATION

Opening Times: The 2nd & 4th Sundays of each month from Easter until October. 2.00pm to 5.00pm. Also open for Birthday parties and Santa Specials.
Steam Working: Every operating day.
Prices: 40p per ride.

Detailed Directions by Car:

Exit the M25 at Junction 14, initially following signs for Heathrow. At the first roundabout, turn left onto the A3044 towards the A4, passing the new Terminal 5 building on the right hand side. On reaching the A4 turn right towards London. After 2½ miles, at Harlington Corner, turn left onto the A437. The Railway is situated in Harlington village centre on the right, approximately 75 yards after crossing over the mini-roundabout.

HILLS MINIATURE RAILWAY

Address: Hills Garden Centre, London Road, Allostock, Knutsford, Cheshire, WA16 9LU
Telephone Nº: (01565) 722567
Year Formed: 2000
Location of Line: Hills Garden Centre

Length of Line: 800 yards
Nº of Steam Locos: 2
Nº of Other Locos: 3
Approx Nº of Visitors P.A.: 12,000
Gauge: 7¼ inches
Web site: www.hills-miniature-railway.co.uk

GENERAL INFORMATION

Nearest Mainline Station: Holmes Chapel (4 miles)
Nearest Bus Station: Holmes Chapel (4 miles)
Car Parking: Spaces for 80 cars on site
Coach Parking: One space available on site
Souvenir Shop(s): Yes
Food & Drinks: Yes

SPECIAL INFORMATION

The Railway runs through the landscaped grounds of the Hills Garden Centre.

OPERATING INFORMATION

Opening Times: The Railway opens on weekends and Bank Holidays throughout the year. Trains run from 10.45am to 4.30pm. All train times are weather permitting.
Steam Working: Daily when operating
Prices: Adult £1.00 per ride
Child 50p per ride (Under-2s free)
10 ride ticket £8.00

Detailed Directions by Car:
From the North & South: Exit the M6 at Junction 18 and follow the A54 to Holmes Chapel. In Holmes Chapel turn left onto the A50 London Road and follow for 5 miles. Hills Garden Centre is on the left hand side.

HOLLYCOMBE STEAM COLLECTION

Address: Hollycombe, Liphook, Hants. GU30 7LP	**N° of Steam Locos**: 3
Telephone N°: (01428) 724900	**N° of Other Locos**: 1
Year Formed: 1970	**N° of Members**: 100
Location of Line: Hollycombe, Liphook	**Annual Membership Fee**: £8.00
Length of Line: 1¾ miles Narrow gauge, ¼ mile Standard gauge	**Approx N° of Visitors P.A.**: 35,000
	Gauge: 2 feet plus Standard & 7¼ inches
	Web site: www.hollycombe.co.uk

GENERAL INFORMATION

Nearest Mainline Station: Liphook (1 mile)
Nearest Bus Station: Liphook
Car Parking: Extensive grass area
Coach Parking: Hardstanding
Souvenir Shop(s): Yes
Food & Drinks: Yes – Cafe

SPECIAL INFORMATION

The narrow gauge railway ascends to spectacular views of the Downs and is part of an extensive working steam museum.

OPERATING INFORMATION

Opening Times: Sundays and Bank Holidays from 1st April to 7th October. Open daily from 29th July to 27th August.
Steam Working: 1.00pm to 5.00pm
Prices: Adult £10.00
           Child £8.50
           Senior Citizen £9.00
           Family £35.00 (2 adults + 3 children)
Note: Prices are £1.00 less on Summer weekdays

Detailed Directions by Car:
Take the A3 to Liphook and follow the brown tourist signs for the railway.

HULL & DISTRICT S.M.E.E.

Address: c/o West Park Bowls Pavilion, Walton Street, Hull HU5 6JU
Phone Nº: (01262) 678767 (Secretary)
Year Formed: 1937
Location of Line: West Park, Hull
Length of Line: 190 metres (raised track) and 400 metres (ground level track)

Nº of Steam Locos: Approximately 15
Nº of Other Locos: Approximately 10
Nº of Members: Approximately 68
Approx Nº of Visitors P.A.: 5,000
Gauge: 2½ inches, 3½ inches & 5 inches on the raised track; 5 inches & 7¼ inches on the ground level track
Web site: www.finnaj.karoo.net/hdsmee.html

GENERAL INFORMATION

Nearest Mainline Station: Hull Paragon (1½ miles)
Nearest Bus Station: Hull Central (1½ miles)
Car Parking: Available on site
Coach Parking: None
Food & Drinks: None

SPECIAL INFORMATION

The Hull & District Society of Model & Experimental Engineers operates a railway in West Park in Hull. A two day steam festival is to be held on 14th and 15th July 2007.

OPERATING INFORMATION

Opening Times: Passenger services run on Wednesdays & Sundays from noon until teatime subject to demand levels and the season. Please contact the Railway for further details.
Steam Working: Whenever available.
Prices: Free of charge but a 20p donation per ride is suggested.

Detailed Directions by Car:
From the West, take the M62 to Hull where it becomes the A63. Continue along the A63 (Clive Sullivan Way) then turn left into Rawling Way following the signs for Hull Royal Infirmary. After ½ mile turn left onto Anlaby Road (A1105) then left after ½ mile into Walton Street. Turn right into West Park then right again for the Railway.

ICKENHAM MINIATURE RAILWAY

Correspondence: 25 Copthall Road East, Ickenham, Middlesex UB10 8SD	**N⁰ of Steam Locos:** Up to 6
Telephone N⁰: (01895) 630125	**N⁰ of Other Locos:** Up to 4
Year Formed: 1948	**N⁰ of Members:** Approximately 70
Location: At the rear of the "Coach and Horses" Public House, Ickenham	**Approx N⁰ of Visitors P.A.:** 9,000
Length of Line: 1,100 feet	**Gauge:** 3½ inches and 5 inches
	Gauge: www.idsme.co.uk

GENERAL INFORMATION

Nearest Mainline Station: West Ruislip (½ mile)
Nearest Bus Station: Uxbridge (2½ miles) – use the U1 or U10 bus services for Ickenham
Car Parking: Public car park is adjacent
Coach Parking: None
Food & Drinks: Available

SPECIAL INFORMATION

The Railway is operated by volunteers from the Ickenham & District Society of Model Engineers.

OPERATING INFORMATION

Opening Times: The first Saturday of the month from April to December inclusive. Trains run from 12.00pm to 5.30pm (or until dusk later in the year).
Steam Working: All operating days subject to availability.
Prices: 40p per ride.

Detailed Directions by Car:
The Railway is located in Ickenham Village behind the Coach and Horses Public House which is adjacent to the junction of the B466 Ickenham High Road, B466 Long Lane and the B467 Swakeleys Road. From the East: Exit the A40 at Hillingdon Circus turning right onto the B466 Long Lane towards Ickenham/Ruislip. Continue for 1 mile and turn right into Community Close for the car park just before the Coach and Horses in the centre of Ickenham; From the West: Exit the A40 at Hillingdon Circus turning left onto B466 Long Lane. Then as above.

ILFORD & WEST ESSEX MODEL RAILWAY CLUB

Address: Station Road, Chadwell Heath, Romford, Essex
Telephone Nº: (01708) 450424
Year Formed: 1930
Location of Line: Chadwell Heath
Length of Line: 150 yards

Nº of Steam Locos: 3
Nº of Other Locos: 2
Nº of Members: Approximately 50
Approx Nº of Visitors P.A.: 400
Gauge: 7¼ inches
Web site: www.iwemrc.org.uk

GENERAL INFORMATION

Nearest Mainline Station: Chadwell Heath
Nearest Bus Station: Chadwell Heath (100 yards)
Car Parking: None on site but a public car park is 100 yards away
Coach Parking: None
Food & Drinks: Light refreshments are available

SPECIAL INFORMATION

The Ilford & West Essex Model Railway Club was formed in 1930 and as such is one of the oldest clubs of its type in the country. Please note that access to the site is by steps only and it is therefore not suitable for wheelchairs.

OPERATING INFORMATION

Opening Times: The first Sunday of the month from April to September inclusive. Trains run from 10.30am to 4.00pm.
Steam Working: All operating days.
Prices: 50p per ride

Detailed Directions by Car:
The site is alongside Chadwell Heath mainline station just off the A118 between Romford and Ilford town centres. Station Road is to the South of the A118 approximately half-way between the two towns. The site itself is approximately 200 yards down Station Road with a car park on the right hand side.

JOCKS LANE RAILWAY

Correspondence: Bracknell Railway Society, Unit 6, Pinewood Centre, Wokingham, Berkshire RG40 3AQ
Telephone Nº: (01344) 420919
Year Formed: 1972
Location of Line: Jocks Lane Park, Bracknell
Length of Line: 1,140 feet

Nº of Steam Locos: 20
Nº of Other Locos: 15
Nº of Members: Approximately 80
Approx Nº of Visitors P.A.: 1,100
Gauge: 3½ inches and 5 inches
Web site: www.bracknellrailwaysociety.co.uk

GENERAL INFORMATION

Nearest Mainline Station: Bracknell (2 miles)
Nearest Bus Station: Bracknell (2 miles)
Car Parking: Available on site
Coach Parking: Available by prior arrangement
Souvenir Shop(s): None
Food & Drinks: Available

SPECIAL INFORMATION

The Jocks Lane Railway is operated by members of the Bracknell Railway Society.

OPERATING INFORMATION

Opening Times: The second Sunday of the month and Bank Holidays from Easter to October. Trains run from 3.00pm to 5.30pm.
Steam Working: All operating days.
Prices: Adults 50p
       Children 50p

Detailed Directions by Car:
From the centre of Bracknell, take the B3018 Binfield Road to the edge of town (signposted for Binfield and Twyford). The Park is signposted on the left – turn into Jocks Lane then right into the car park at the road barrier; From Wokingham follow the B3408 (London Road) to Bracknell then take the 2nd exit at the roundabout into Temple Way. Take the 2nd exit at the Temple Park Roundabout into Binfield Road, the 2nd exit at Framptons Bridge Roundabout and then the first turning on the right into Jocks Lane for the park.

KEIGHLEY & DISTRICT M.E.S.

Correspondence: 48 Park Road, Bingley, West Yorkshire	**N° of Steam Locos**: 8
Telephone N°: (01274) 564866	**N° of Other Locos**: 5
Year Formed: 1950	**N° of Members**: Approximately 80
Location of Line: Marley Sports Centre, Keighley	**Approx N° of Visitors P.A.**: 500 – 1,000
Length of Line: 1,500 feet	**Gauge**: 3½ inches and 5 inches

GENERAL INFORMATION

Nearest Mainline Station: Keighley (1 mile)
Nearest Bus Station: Keighley (1½ miles)
Car Parking: Available on site
Coach Parking: None
Food & Drinks: Available

SPECIAL INFORMATION

Keighley & District Model Engineering Society holds regular public open days at their railway which is situated by the Marley Leisure Centre in Keighley. Please contact the Society for further details.

OPERATING INFORMATION

Opening Times: Open days are held on some Sundays. Please contact the Society for dates. Trains run from 1.30pm to 5.00pm on these days.
Steam Working: All operating days.
Prices: 30p per person for two circuits of the track.

Detailed Directions by Car:
From Bradford: Take the A650 towards Keighley. Upon reaching Keighley (with the Marley Leisure Centre on the right) take the 4th exit at the roundabout into the car park then follow the signs for the railway; From Skipton: Take the A629 and follow signs for Bradford onto Aire Valley Road. Pass the Beeches Hotel on the right and take the 2nd exit at the next roundabout into the Leisure Centre Car Park for the railway.

King's Lynn & District s.m.e.

Address: Lynnsport, Green Park Avenue, King's Lynn, Norfolk PE30 2NB	**No of Steam Locos**: 6
Telephone No: (01366) 381182	**No of Other Locos**: 11
Year Formed: 1972	**No of Members**: 52
Location of Line: King's Lynn	**Annual Membership Fee**: £17.00 Adult
Length of Line: 627 feet	**Approx No of Visitors P.A.**: Not known
	Gauge: 3½ inches, 5 inches & 7¼ inches
	Web site: www.kldsme.org.uk

GENERAL INFORMATION

Nearest Mainline Station: King's Lynn (2 miles)
Nearest Bus Station: King's Lynn (3 miles)
Car Parking: Available on site
Coach Parking: Available
Food & Drinks: Available in Lynnsport

SPECIAL INFORMATION

The King's Lynn & District Society of Model Engineers first operated a railway in 1972 and the current track at Lynnsport has been working since 1992. Improvements to the Lynnsport facilities have been ongoing ever since.

OPERATING INFORMATION

Opening Times: Every Sunday from Easter until the end of October. Trains run from 12.00pm to 5.00pm
Steam Working: Most operating days.
Prices: 50p per ride.

Detailed Directions by Car:
Lynnsport is well-signposted from the outskirts of King's Lynn so it is easy to find just by following the signs. The railway itself is signposted once in the Lynnsport car park.

KINVER & WEST MIDLANDS S.M.E.

Correspondence: 24 Goodrest Avenue,
Halesowen, West Midlands   B62 0HP
Telephone Nº: (0121) 602-2019
Year Formed: 1961
Location of Line: Kinver, Staffordshire
Length of Line: ½ mile

Nº of Steam Locos: Members locos only
Nº of Other Locos: Members locos only
Nº of Members: Approximately 140
Approx Nº of Visitors P.A.: Not known
Gauge: 3½ inches and 5 inches
Web site: www.kinvermodelengineers.org.uk

GENERAL INFORMATION

Nearest Mainline Station: Kidderminster (6 miles)
Nearest Bus Station: Stourbridge (3 miles)
Car Parking: Available on site
Coach Parking: Available on site
Food & Drinks: None

SPECIAL INFORMATION

The Kinver & West Midlands Society of Model
Engineers dates back to organisations formed in the
1920s and has operated a railway in Kinver since
1962. In addition to the current line a new 7¼ inch
track is nearing completion at this site.

OPERATING INFORMATION

Opening Times: Sunday afternoons between Easter
and October, weather permitting. Trains run
between 2.00pm and 5.00pm.
Steam Working: Most operating days.
Prices: £1.00 per ride.

Detailed Directions by Car:
The Society's tracksite is situated on the Marsh Playing Fields at the end of the High Street in the village of Kinver
which is to the West of Stourbridge and to the North of Kidderminster.

LANGFORD & BEELEIGH RAILWAY

Address: Museum of Power,
Hatfield Road, Langford, Maldon, Essex,
CM9 6QA
Telephone Nº: (01621) 843183
Year Formed: 1999
Location of Line: Langford, Essex
Length of Line: ½ mile loop

Nº of Steam Locos: 2
Nº of Other Locos: 2
Nº of Members: Approximately 160
Approx Nº of Visitors P.A.: 6,000
Gauge: 7¼ inches
Web site: www.museumofpower.org.uk

GENERAL INFORMATION

Nearest Mainline Station: Witham (4 miles)
Nearest Bus Station: Chelmsford (6 miles)
Car Parking: Available on site
Coach Parking: Available
Souvenir Shop(s): Yes
Food & Drinks: Available

SPECIAL INFORMATION

The Railway is situated at the Museum of Power
which is housed in the Steam Pumping Station at
Langford in Essex. The Museum was set up to
exhibit and demonstrate working examples of power
sources of all types and chronicle the major roles
that they have played in history.

OPERATING INFORMATION

Opening Times: The Museum is open Friday to
Sunday from November to Easter (11.00am to
4.00pm) and Wednesday to Sunday (10.00am to
5.00pm) throughout the rest of the year.
Trains run on the first Sunday of each month from
April to October inclusive. Also during Special
events at various other times of the year. Please
contact the Museum for further information.
Steam Working: Only guaranteed on special event
days although steam will be working at some other
times. 2007 dates: 11th & 18th March; 8th April;
3rd June; 1st July; 16th September; 8th & 9th
December and also 1st January 2008.
Prices: £1.00 per ride.
Note: Admission to the Museum is an extra charge.

Detailed Directions by Car:
The Museum is situated in Langford, on the B1019 Maldon to Hatfield Peverel Road. From the A12, take the
Hatfield Peverel exit, pass through the village and take the B1019 Hatfield Road towards Ulting & Maldon. The
Museum is on the right hand side after approximately 3 miles on the outskirts of Langford.

Littledown Miniature Railway

Address: Littledown Park, Chaseside, Bournemouth BH7 7DX	**Nº of Steam Locos:** 15+
Telephone Nº: None	**Nº of Other Locos:** 10+
Year Formed: 1927	**Nº of Members:** 120+
Location of Line: Littledown Park	**Approx Nº of Visitors P.A.:** 4,000
Length of Line: Over one third of a mile	**Gauge:** 3½ inches, 5 inches & 7¼ inches
	Web site: www.littledownrailway.co.uk

GENERAL INFORMATION

Nearest Mainline Station: Bournemouth Central (3½ miles)
Nearest Bus Station: Bournemouth
Car Parking: In Littledown Leisure Centre car park
Coach Parking: As above

SPECIAL INFORMATION

Bournemouth and District Society of Model Engineers operate the railway at Littledown Park.

OPERATING INFORMATION

Opening Times: Most Sundays and Wednesdays throughout the year subject to weather conditions. Trains run from 11.00am to 3.00pm.
Steam Working: Subject to availability. Please contact the railway for further details.
Prices: £1.00 per ride.

Detailed Directions by Car:
The Railway is situated at Littledown Park which is to the North-East of Bournemouth town centre close (and to the South of) the junction of Wessex Way (A338) and Castle Lane (A3060).

MOORS VALLEY RAILWAY

Address: Moors Valley Country Park, Horton Road, Ashley Heath, Nr. Ringwood, Hants. BH24 2ET **Telephone Nº**: (01425) 471415 **Year Formed**: 1985 **Location of Line**: Moors Valley Country Park	**Length of Line**: 1 mile **Nº of Steam Locos**: 15 **Nº of Other Locos**: 2 **Nº of Members**: – **Approx Nº of Visitors P.A.**: – **Gauge**: 7¼ inches **Web site**: www.moorsvalleyrailway.co.uk

GENERAL INFORMATION

Nearest Mainline Station: Bournemouth (12 miles)
Nearest Bus Station: Ringwood (3 miles)
Car Parking: Parking charges vary throughout the year. Maximum charge £7.00 per day.
Coach Parking: Charges are applied for parking
Souvenir Shop(s): Yes + Model Railway Shop
Food & Drinks: Yes

SPECIAL INFORMATION

The Moors Valley Railway is a complete small Railway with signalling and 2 signal boxes and also 4 tunnels and 2 level crossings.

OPERATING INFORMATION

Opening Times: Weekends throughout the year. Daily from one week before to one week after Easter, Spring Bank Holiday to mid-September, during School half-term holidays and also from Boxing Day to end of School holidays. Also Santa Specials in December and occasional other openings. Phone the Railways for details.
Steam Working: 10.45am to 5.00pm when open.
Prices: Adult Return £2.60;   Adult Single £1.50
      Child Return £1.90;   Child Single £1.05
Special rates are available for parties of 10 or more.

Detailed Directions by Car:
From All Parts: Moors Valley Country Park is situated on Horton Road which is off the A31 Ferndown to Ringwood road near the junction with the A338 to Bournemouth.

NORTHAMPTON SOCIETY OF MODEL ENGINEERS

Correspondence: Hon. Secretary,
Oakwood, 129a High Street, Riseley,
Bedford MK44 1DJ
Telephone Nº: (01234) 708501
Year Formed: 1933
Location of Line: Lower Delapre Park,
London Road, Northampton

Length of Line: 1,010 feet (raised track)
and 1,700 feet (ground level track)
Nº of Steam Locos: Up to 5 running
Nº of Other Locos: 1 or 2 run occasionally
Nº of Members: 86
Approx Nº of Visitors P.A.: 2,000
Gauge: 3½ inches, 5 inches & 7¼ inches
Web site: www.nsme.co.uk

GENERAL INFORMATION

Nearest Mainline Station: Northampton (2 miles)
Nearest Bus Station: Northampton (2 miles)
Car Parking: Available on site
Coach Parking: On London Road
Food & Drinks: Light refreshments are available

SPECIAL INFORMATION

The Northampton Society of Model Engineers is a
long established society with excellent facilities for
model engineers. The society has over 80 members
with wide ranging interests, several of whom have
won major awards at National exhibitions.

OPERATING INFORMATION

Opening Times: May Day Bank Holiday Monday
then the first Sunday of the month thereafter up to
and including October. Trains run from 2.00pm to
5.00pm.
Steam Working: Every operating day.
Prices: 50p per ride.

Detailed Directions by Car:
From the M1: Exit at Junction 15 and take the A508 to Northampton. Take the 2nd turn off onto the A45 (for the
Town Centre) and then the 2nd exit at the roundabout. After ½ mile turn right just before the pelican crossing
and immediately turn left through the steel gate onto the access track for the railway; From the East: Follow the
A45 and take the turn off signposted for Daventry and the Town Centre. Take the 4th exit at the roundabout onto
the A508, then as above; From the Town Centre: Take the A508 South (Bridge Street). Cross the river and go
straight on at the traffic lights. Pass a petrol station on the left and immediately after the pelican crossing turn left
then immediately left again for the railway.

NORTHOLT MODEL RAILWAY CLUB

Address: Northolt Village Community
Centre, Ealing Road, Northolt,
Middlesex   UB5 6AD
Phone Nº: (01753) 652678 (Secretary)
Year Formed: 1950
Location of Line: Northolt, Middlesex
Length of Line: 680 feet

Nº of Steam Locos: 10
Nº of Other Locos: 1
Nº of Members: 60+
Approx Nº of Visitors P.A.: 300
Gauge: 3½ inches and 5 inches
Web site: www.northolt-mrc.org.uk

GENERAL INFORMATION

Nearest Mainline Station: Greenford (1 mile)
Nearest Tube Station: Northolt (½ mile)
Car Parking: Street parking only
Coach Parking: None
Food & Drinks: Light refreshments available

SPECIAL INFORMATION

Northolt Model Railway Club was formed in 1950
and has its permanent accommodation situated
within the Northolt Village Community Centre. The
track, which runs around the Community Centre
perimeter, was built between 1962 and 1965.

OPERATING INFORMATION

Opening Times: 2007 dates: 15th April, 20th May,
17th June, 15th July, 19th August, 16th September.
Trains run from 2.00pm to 5.00pm.
Steam Working: Every operational day.
Prices: 25p per ride.

Detailed Directions by Car:
Exit the A40 at the Target roundabout and follow signs, heading northwards, for Northolt on the A312 Church
Road. Take the third turning on the right (also Church Road) and turn right again at the bottom of the road and
the Community Centre and its grounds can be seen on the right hand side. Street parking only is available.

NORTH NORFOLK MODEL ENGINEERING CLUB

Address: c/o Holt Station, Cromer Road, Holt, Norfolk
Telephone Nº: None
Year Formed: 1992
Location of Line: Holt Station Yard
Length of Line: 1,000 feet

Nº of Steam Locos: 10
Nº of Other Locos: 8
Nº of Members: Approximately 45
Approx Nº of Visitors P.A.: 2,000
Gauge: 3½ inches and 5 inches

GENERAL INFORMATION

Nearest Mainline Station: Sheringham (6 miles)
Nearest Bus Stop: 300 yards
Car Parking: Available on site
Coach Parking: None
Souvenir Shop(s): In Holt Station
Food & Drinks: Snacks from Holt Station shop

SPECIAL INFORMATION

North Norfolk Model Engineering Club operates a miniature railway in the yard of Holt Station on the North Norfolk Railway. For details about the NNR please phone (01263) 820800 or check their web site: www.nnr.co.uk

OPERATING INFORMATION

Opening Times: Most Sunday afternoons from April to October inclusive. However, this depends on the availability of drivers, locos and the weather! Also open during most North Norfolk Railway special events.
Steam Working: Most Sundays during the Summer and also during NNR special events.
Prices: No charge but donations are appreciated.

Detailed Directions by Car:
The miniature railway is situated in the yard of Holt Station which is by the side of the A148 Cromer to Fakenham road between the villages of Holt and High Kelling.

NORTH SCARLE MINIATURE RAILWAY

Address: North Scarle Playing Field, Swinderby Road, North Scarle, Lincolnshire
Telephone Nº: (01522) 888228
Year Formed: 1933
Location of Line: North Scarle, between Newark and Lincoln
Length of Line: A third of a mile

Nº of Steam Locos: 7
Nº of Other Locos: 5
Nº of Members: 45
Annual Membership Fee: £25.00
Approx Nº of Visitors P.A.: 3,000
Gauges: 7¼ inches and 5 inches

GENERAL INFORMATION

Nearest Mainline Station: Newark Northgate (5 miles)
Nearest Bus Station: Newark (5 miles)
Car Parking: 300 spaces available on site
Coach Parking: None available
Souvenir Shop(s): None
Food & Drinks: Available on special days only

SPECIAL INFORMATION

The Railway is owned and operated by the Lincoln and District Model Engineering Society which was founded in 1933.

OPERATING INFORMATION

Opening Times: Car Boot Sale Sundays only!
Dates for 2007: 25th March; 8th & 22nd April; 6th & 20th May; 3rd & 17th June; 1st, 15th & 29th July; 12th & 26th August; 9th, 15th, 16th (Special Open Weekend with miniature steam rally including traction engines) & 23rd September; 7th October.
Steam Working: Every running day.
Prices: Adult Return 50p
         Child Return 50p

Detailed Directions by Car:
North Scarle is situated off the A46 between Lincoln and Newark (about 5 miles from Newark). Alternatively, take the A1133 from Gainsborough and follow the North Scarle signs when around 6 miles from Newark.

NORWICH & DISTRICT S.M.E.

Correspondence Address: 'Timberlee', Bungay Road, Scole, Diss   IP21 4DX
Telephone Nº: (01379) 740578
Year Formed: 1933
Location of Line: Eaton Park, Norwich
Length of Line: Two tracks – one of 800 metres and one of 955 feet

Nº of Steam Locos: 5
Nº of Other Locos: 2
Nº of Members: Approximately 120
Approx Nº of Visitors P.A.: 8,000
Gauge: 3½ inches, 5 inches & 7¼ inches

GENERAL INFORMATION

Nearest Mainline Station: Norwich (3 miles)
Nearest Bus Station: Norwich (2 miles)
Car Parking: Available in Eaton Park
Coach Parking: None
Food & Drinks: None

SPECIAL INFORMATION

Norwich & District Society of Model Engineers was formed in 1933 and operates two tracks in Eaton Park, one raised and the other ground level.

OPERATING INFORMATION

Opening Times: Sundays during the busy season. Trains run from 2.00pm to 5.00pm. Please contact the railway for further details.
Steam Working: Every operating day.
Prices: £1.00 per ride on the long track
50p per ride on the short track

Detailed Directions by Car:
Take the A11 or A140 into Norwich and upon reaching the ring road, turn left. At the second set of traffic lights turn left into South Park Avenue and the entrance to Eaton Park is on the right hand side.
Alternative route: Take the A47 into Norwich and turn right at the ring road. At the 3rd set of traffic lights turn right into South Park Avenue.

NOTTINGHAM S.M.E.E

Address: Nottingham Transport Heritage Centre, Mere Way, Ruddington, Nottingham NG11 6NX	**Nº of Steam Locos**: Several
	Nº of Other Locos: Several
	Nº of Members: Approximately 180
Telephone Nº: None	**Approx Nº of Visitors P.A.**: 12,000
Year Formed: 1929	**Gauge**: 3½ inches, 5 inches & 7¼ inches
Location of Line: Nottingham Transport Heritate Centre, Ruddington	**Web site**: www.nsmee.com
Length of Line: ½ mile	

GENERAL INFORMATION

Nearest Mainline Station: Nottingham (5 miles)
Nearest Bus Station: Bus service from Nottingham to the Centre
Car Parking: Free parking at site
Coach Parking: Free parking at site
Souvenir Shop(s): Yes
Food & Drinks: Yes

SPECIAL INFORMATION

The Nottingham Society of Model & Experimental Engineers relocated to the Nottingham Heritage Centre in 1992 and have since spent thousands of man-hours constructing multiple tracks for different train gauges.

OPERATING INFORMATION

Opening Times: Sundays from Easter until the end of September. Open 10.00am to 4.30pm.
Steam Working: Most services are steam-hauled.
Prices: Adults 40p per ride
    Children 30p per ride

Detailed Directions by Car:
From All Parts: The centre is situated off the A60 Nottingham to Loughborough Road and is signposted just south of the traffic lights at Ruddington.

ORCHID LINE MINIATURE RAILWAY

Address: Curraghs Wildlife Park, Ballaugh, Isle of Man **Telephone Nº:** (01624) 897323 **Year Formed:** 1992 **Location:** Within the Wildlife Park **Length of Line:** 1,000 yards	**Nº of Steam Locos:** 10 **Nº of Other Locos:** 2 **Nº of Members:** Approximately 85 **Approx Nº of Visitors P.A.:** 15,000 **Gauge:** 3½ inches, 5 inches & 7¼ inches **Web sites:** www.gov.im/wildlife www.homepages.mcb.net/howe/msmec.htm

GENERAL INFORMATION

Nearest Bus Station: At the Wildlife Park
Car Parking: Available on site
Coach Parking: Available
Souvenir Shop(s): Yes
Food & Drinks: Available

SPECIAL INFORMATION

The Railway is operated by members of the Manx Steam & Model Engineering Club. Please note that an entrance fee is charged to enter the Wildlife Park and this is required to access the railway.

OPERATING INFORMATION

Railway Opening Times: Sundays and Bank Holidays from Easter to October. Also open on Saturdays during the school holidays. Trains run from 12.00pm to 4.30pm.
Steam Working: Most operating days.
Prices: 50p per ride
Note: The above price does not include the entrance fee for the Wildlife Park.

Detailed Directions by Car:
Curraghs Wildlife Park lies on the main road between Ramsey and Ballaugh and is well-signposted.

PAPPLEWICK PUMPING STATION

<table>
<tr><td>

Address: Papplewick Pumping Station,
Off Longdale Lane, Ravenshead,
Nottingham   NG15 9AJ
Telephone Nº: (0115) 963-2938
Year Formed: 1978
Location: Papplewick Pumping Station
Length of Line: 250 metres

</td><td>

Nº of Steam Locos: 1+ visiting locos only
Nº of Other Locos: 1
Nº of Members: –
Approx Nº of Visitors P.A.: Not known
Gauge: 7¼ inches
Web site:
www.papplewickpumpingstation.co.uk

</td></tr>
</table>

GENERAL INFORMATION

Nearest Mainline Station: Hucknall (3½ miles)
Nearest Bus Station: Hucknall
Car Parking: Available on site
Coach Parking: Available on site
Souvenir Shop(s): Yes
Food & Drinks: Available

SPECIAL INFORMATION

The Pumping Station railway is operated by
members of the Chesterfield & District Model
Engineering Society. Papplewick Pumping Station is
Britain's finest Victorian Water Works and the only
one in the Midlands to be preserved as a complete
working water pumping station.

OPERATING INFORMATION

Opening Times: The Pumping Station itself is open
for static viewing on Sunday afternoons (12.00pm to
4.00pm) from February to October. The Beam
Engines and train rides only operate on certain
dates. See below for 2007 dates.

Steam Working: 8th & 9th April; 6th, 7th, 27th &
28th May; 14th & 15th July; 26th & 27th August;
15h & 16th September; 20th & 21st October;
29th & 30th December. Steam working from
11.00am to 5.00pm on Sundays and Mondays and
from 1.00pm to 5.00pm on Saturdays.

Prices: Adults £4.80   (Static days £3.00)
         Children £2.80   (Static days £2.00)
         Concessions £3.80
         Family £13.50

Detailed Directions by Car:
Papplewick Pumping Station is situated 3 miles to the North of the village of Papplewick, off the A60 Mansfield to
Nottingham road. Turn off the A60 following signs for Burntstump Country Park/Police Headquarters. Pass
both of these and continue left over the railway line. Look for the Pumping Station's chimney.

PINEWOOD MINIATURE RAILWAY

Address: Pinewood Leisure Centre, Old Wokingham Road, Wokingham, Berkshire   RG40 3AQ
Phone Nº: (01252) 510340 (Secretary)
Year Formed: 1984
Location: Pinewood Leisure Centre
Length of Line: 700 metres

Nº of Steam Locos: 50   (All owned
Nº of Other Locos: 30   by Members)
Nº of Members: Approximately 50
Annual Membership Fee: £35.00
Approx Nº of Visitors P.A.: 2,500
Gauge: 5 inches and 7¼ inches
Web site: www.pinewoodrailway.co.uk

GENERAL INFORMATION

Nearest Mainline Station: Bracknell
Nearest Bus Station: Bracknell
Car Parking: Available on site
Coach Parking: Available by arrangement
Souvenir Shop(s): None
Food & Drinks: Tea/Coffee making facilities only

SPECIAL INFORMATION

The Pinewood Miniature Railway runs through attractive woodlands backing on to a Leisure Centre.

OPERATING INFORMATION

Opening Times: Year-round work sessions on Sunday mornings and all day on Wednesdays.
Steam Working: Members Steam Up on 1st Sunday of the month. Public running on the 3rd Sunday in the month from April to October (November if the weather is fine). Santa Specials on some dates in December (pre-booking is advised). Private Parties can sometimes be catered for by prior arrangement.
Prices: 70p per ride

Detailed Directions by Car:
From the M3 or the A30 take the A322 towards Bracknell. Once on the A322, keep in the left hand lane to the first major roundabout then take the first exit onto the B3430 towards Wokingham along Nine Mile Ride. Cross the next roundabout (A3095) and continue on the B3430 passing the Golden Retriever pub and the Crematorium. Go straight on at the next mini-roundabout then turn right at the following roundabout into Old Wokingham Road. The Pinewood Leisure Centre is on the left after approximately 100 metres.

PLYMOUTH MINIATURE STEAM

Address: Goodwin Park,
Pendeen Crescent, Southway, Plymouth
Phone Nº: (01752) 201771 (Secretary)
Year Formed: 1970
Location of Line: Goodwin Park Public
Nature Reserve
Length of Line: ½ mile

Nº of Steam Locos: 2 + member locos
Nº of Other Locos: 2 + member locos
Nº of Members: Approximately 100
Approx Nº of Visitors P.A.: 2,000
Gauge: 3½ inches, 5 inches & 7¼ inches
Web site:
members.lycos.co.uk/Plym_Min_Steam/

GENERAL INFORMATION

Nearest Mainline Station: Plymouth (6 miles)
Nearest Bus Station: Plymouth (6 miles)
Car Parking: Available on site
Coach Parking: None
Food & Drinks: Light refreshments available.

SPECIAL INFORMATION

The railway runs through Goodwin Park, a site
specially developed by members of the Society
which was opened in 1990 and has since been
designated as a Public Nature Reserve.

OPERATING INFORMATION

Opening Times: Open during the 1st and 3rd
Sunday afternoons of each month from April to
October inclusive.
Steam Working: Most operating days.
Prices: 50 per ride.

Detailed Directions by Car:
From the A38 Plymouth Parkway, follow the signs for Tavistock (A386) travelling North until reaching a new
road junction near Plymouth Airport and a Park & Ride site. Turn left at this junction into the Southway Estate
and follow the road for ½ mile past two mini-roundabouts and a set of traffic lights. At the 3rd mini-roundabout
turn left into Pendeen Crescent and about 200 yard on the right is a signpost for the railway. Follow the lane to the
parking area but please note that the bridge has just 6 feet headroom so large vehicles must park elsewhere!

PURBECK MINIATURE RAILWAY

Address: Purbeck School, Wareham, Dorset BH20 4PF
Contact Telephone N°: (01929) 556031
Year Formed: 1989
Location of Line: In the grounds of Purbeck School
Length of Line: 245 metres

N° of Steam Locos: 6
N° of Other Locos: 6
N° of Members: 12
Approx N° of Visitors P.A.: Not known
Gauge: 7¼ inches

GENERAL INFORMATION

Nearest Mainline Station: Wareham (1 mile)
Nearest Bus Station: Wareham (1 mile)
Car Parking: Available on site
Coach Parking: Available
Food & Drinks: Light refreshments available

SPECIAL INFORMATION

The railway usually operates during Car Boot events held at the school and boarding is at Monument Station in the car park. The outward journey runs through the school grounds, across a wildlife pond, through a tunnel and into the main station where visitors can view the engine sheds. A different engine is then coupled to the train for the return journey.

OPERATING INFORMATION

Opening Times: The first Sunday of the month from March to December but excluding August when the school is closed for the Summer. Trains run from 9.00am to 1.00pm.
Steam Working: Every operating day.
Prices: 50p per ride on normal running days
£1.00 per ride on Special Event days

Detailed Directions by Car:
Wareham can be approached via the A352 Dorchester road or the A351 Poole to Swanage road. The Purbeck School is situated adjacent to the main roundabout where the A351 and A352 meet.

RIBBLE VALLEY LIVE STEAMERS

Address: Edisford Bridge, Edisford Road,
Clitheroe, Lancashire
Phone Nº: (01254) 385170 (Secretary)
Year Formed: 1947
Location of Line: Edisford Bridge
Length of Line: 1,250 feet

Nº of Steam Locos: 10
Nº of Other Locos: 8
Nº of Members: Approximately 35
Approx Nº of Visitors P.A.: Not known
Gauge: 2½ inches, 3½ inches & 5 inches

GENERAL INFORMATION

Nearest Mainline Station: Clitheroe (1 mile)
Nearest Bus Station: Clitheroe (1 mile)
Car Parking: Disabled parking only on site but
there is a car park on the main road nearby.
Coach Parking: None
Souvenir Shop(s): Yes
Food & Drinks: Available

SPECIAL INFORMATION

The railway is situated by Edisford Bridge, which
dates as far back as the 14th Century.

OPERATING INFORMATION

Opening Times: Most weekends from Easter until
the end of September and also some weekdays
during the school holidays. Please contact the
railway for further details.
Steam Working: Every operating day.
Prices: 40p for 2 laps of the track.

Detailed Directions by Car:
The railway is situated 1 mile to the West of Clitheroe on the B6243 by Edisford Bridge and between the caravan
park and the River Ribble.

ROXBOURNE PARK MINIATURE RAILWAY

Address: Roxbourne Park,
Field End Road, Eastcote, Middlesex
Telephone Nº: None
Year Formed: 1936
Location of Line: Roxbourne Park
Length of Line: 2,200 feet

Nº of Steam Locos: Members locos only
Nº of Other Locos: Members locos only
Nº of Members: Approximately 100
Approx Nº of Visitors P.A.: 2,500
Gauge: 3½ inches, 5 inches & 7¼ inches
Web site: www.hwsme.org.uk

GENERAL INFORMATION

Nearest Tube Station: Eastcote (½ mile)
Nearest Bus Station: –
Car Parking: Available on site
Coach Parking: None
Food & Drinks: None

SPECIAL INFORMATION

The railway is operated by members of the Harrow & Wembley Society of Model Engineers which has been running passenger services on the current track in Roxbourne Park since 1979.

OPERATING INFORMATION

Opening Times: Every Sunday from 1st April to 21st October inclusive. Trains run from 2.30pm to 5.30pm.
Steam Working: Every operating day.
Prices: 50p per ride.

Detailed Directions by Car:
Exit the M40 at Target roundabout and travel into Northolt Village on the A312. Turn left into Eastcote Lane North after the traffic lights just after Northolt Station and continue along this road. Eastcote Lane becomes Field End Road and Roxbourne Park is a little further on opposite Venue '5' (formerly The Clay Pigeon Public House).

Saffron Walden & District S.M.E.

Correspondence: The Secretary, 229 Ramsgate Road, Broadstairs, Kent
Telephone Nº: (01843) 596822
Year Formed: 1980
Location of Line: Audley End Miniature Railway
Length of Line: 1,500 feet

Nº of Steam Locos: 5
Nº of Other Locos: 5
Nº of Members: Approximately 45
Approx Nº of Visitors P.A.: 1,500
Gauge: 3½ inches, 5 inches & 7¼ inches
Web site: www.swdsme.org.uk

GENERAL INFORMATION

Nearest Mainline Station: Audley End (1 mile)
Nearest Bus Station: Saffron Walden (1 mile)
Car Parking: Available on site
Coach Parking: Available on site
Souvenir Shop(s): Yes
Food & Drinks: Snacks available

SPECIAL INFORMATION

The Saffron Walden & District Society of Model Engineers uses a track at Audley End Steam Railway, Lord Braybrooke's private 10¼ inch railway situated just next to Audley End House, an English Heritage site.

OPERATING INFORMATION

Opening Times: Most Sundays from April to October inclusive. Trains run from 2.00pm to 5.00pm.
Steam Working: Most operating days.
Prices: £1.00 per ride (A Multi-ticket is £3.00)

Detailed Directions by Car:
Exit the M11 at Junction 10 if southbound or Junction 9 if northbound and follow the signs for Audley End House. The railway is situated just across the road from Audley End House.

SOUTH DURHAM S.M.E.

Address: Hurworth Grange Community Centre, 41 Croft Road, Hurworth, Darlington DL2 2BN
Phone Nº: (01325) 721503 (Secretary)
Year Formed: 1969
Location of Line: Hurworth
Length of Line: 730 yards

Nº of Steam Locos: 7
Nº of Other Locos: 2
Nº of Members: Approximately 30
Approx Nº of Visitors P.A.: Not known
Gauge: 3½ inches, 5 inches & 7¼ inches
Web site: www.sdsme.co.uk

GENERAL INFORMATION

Nearest Mainline Station: Darlington (3 miles)
Nearest Bus Station: Darlington (3 miles)
Car Parking: Free parking available on site
Coach Parking: Free parking available on site
Food & Drinks: None

SPECIAL INFORMATION

The South Durham Society of Model Engineers has been resident at the Hurworth Grange Centre since 1969. The Society has recently rebuilt the outside-elevated locomotive track which runs through the grounds of the Grange.

OPERATING INFORMATION

Opening Times: First Sunday of the month throughout the year, weather permitting. Trains run from 10.30am to 3.00pm. Please phone to check the railway is operating if the weather is bad.
Steam Working: Every operating day.
Prices: 50p per ride.

Detailed Directions by Car:
Hurworth is a village just to the South of Darlington which is situated on the A167 Northallerton road. Travelling from Darlington, turn left at Hurworth Place, just before Croft Bridge. The Hurworth Grange Community Centre is signposted off the main road through the village, opposite the Comprehensive School.

Spenborough M.E.E.

Contact Address: F. Harrison (Secretary),
20 Victoria Terrace, Cleckheaton,
BD19 3BH
Telephone Nº: (01274) 861631
Year Formed: 1950
Location: Royds Park, Spenborough
Length of Line: One tenth of a mile

Nº of Steam Locos: 2 (+ members locos)
Nº of Other Locos: Various
Nº of Members: 24
Approx Nº of Visitors P.A.: 2,000
Gauge: 2½ inches, 3½ inches, 5 inches
and 7¼ inches

GENERAL INFORMATION

Nearest Mainline Station: Dewsbury (5 miles)
Nearest Bus Station: Cleckheaton
Car Parking: Approximately 20 spaces on site
Coach Parking: None
Food & Drinks: Light refreshments available

SPECIAL INFORMATION

Spenborough Model & Experimental Engineers
operate their service on a track in Royds Park which
is built on the trackbed of the old London & North
West Railway.

OPERATING INFORMATION

Opening Times: The 2nd and 4th Sunday of the
month from May to October inclusive plus certain
extra days in August. Please contact the railway for
further details.
Steam Working: Most operating days.
Prices: 50p per ride.

Detailed Directions by Car:
Exit the M62 at Junction 26 and turn off at the roundabout onto the A638 Cleckheaton to Dewsbury road. Travel
through Cleckheaton for approximately ¾ mile then, just after the start of the dual carriageway, turn left onto
New Street and at the top of the street is the entrance to Royds Park.

SUMMERFIELD FARM RAILWAY

Address: Summerfield Farm, Haynes, Bedford	**Nº of Steam Locos:** 8
	Nº of Other Locos: 7
Telephone Nº: (01234) 301867	**Nº of Members:** Approximately 200
Year Formed: 1992	**Annual Membership Fee:** £25.00
Location: Off the A600, North of Haynes	**Approx Nº of Visitors P.A.:** 10,000
Length of Line: Approximately ¾ mile	**Gauge:** 7¼ inches

GENERAL INFORMATION

Nearest Mainline Station: Bedford (5½ miles)
Nearest Bus Station: Bedford
Car Parking: Available on site
Coach Parking: Available on site
Souvenir Shop(s): None
Food & Drinks: Available

SPECIAL INFORMATION

Summerfield Farm Railway is operated by the Bedford Model Engineering Society.

OPERATING INFORMATION

Opening Times: Opening times vary – please phone for details.
Steam Working: On all public running days
Prices: Adult Return £1.50
Child Return £1.50

Detailed Directions by Car:
From All Parts: The Railway is located by the A600 just to the North of Haynes, 5½ miles South of Bedford and 3½ miles North of Shefford.

Surrey Society of Model Engineers

Address: Mill Lane, Leatherhead, Surrey
Telephone No: None
Year Formed: 1978
Location of Line: Mill Lane, Leatherhead
Length of Line: 2,000 feet

No of Steam Locos: 10
No of Other Locos: 8
No of Members: 52
Approx No of Visitors P.A.: 10,000
Gauge: Both ground and raised level tracks are available covering many gauges
Web site: www.ssme.co.uk

GENERAL INFORMATION

Nearest Mainline Station: Leatherhead (½ mile)
Nearest Bus Station: Leatherhead (½ mile)
Car Parking: Parking on a grass area is possible when conditions allow
Coach Parking: None
Food & Drinks: Available

OPERATING INFORMATION

Opening Times: Various Bank Holidays on other dates throughout the year. 2007 dates: 1st January, 6th April, 7th & 28th May, 23rd June, 8th July, 12th & 27th August, 9th September, 7th October and Santa Specials on 8th & 9th December. Trains run from 11.00am to 4.00pm. Please contact the railway or check their web site for further details.
Steam Working: All operating days.
Prices: £1.00 per ride
£5.00 multi-ride ticket allows 6 rides
Note: Pre-bookings are required for Santa Specials

Detailed Directions by Car:
The railway is situated near Leatherhead town centre. Mill Lane is across the road from the well signposted Leisure Centre just off the B2122 Waterway Road and just a short walk to the south of Leatherhead Mainline station.

THAMES DITTON MINIATURE RAILWAY

Address: Claygate Lane, Thames Ditton, Surrey
Telephone Nº: None
Year Formed: 1936
Location of Line: Thames Ditton
Length of Line: ½ mile

Nº of Steam Locos: 20
Nº of Other Locos: 7
Nº of Members: Approximately 200
Approx Nº of Visitors P.A.: 15,000
Gauge: 3½ inches, 5 inches & 7¼ inches
Web site: www.malden-dsme.co.uk

GENERAL INFORMATION

Nearest Mainline Station: Thames Ditton (½ mile)
Nearest Bus Station: Thames Ditton
Car Parking: Street parking only
Coach Parking: None
Souvenir Shop(s): Yes
Food & Drinks: Available

SPECIAL INFORMATION

The Railway is operated by members of the Malden & District Society of Model Engineers. On open days rides depart every few minutes on two separate tracks which run through the Claygate Lane site.

OPERATING INFORMATION

Opening Times: Open on the first Sunday of each month from Easter to October and also on Bank Holiday Sundays and Mondays. Trains run from 2.00pm to 5.30pm though the site is open from 1.00pm onwards.
Steam Working: Every operating day.
Prices: Adults £5.00
Children £2.00
Family £15.00)

Detailed Directions by Car:
Claygate Lane is located just off the A307 Escher to Kingston road about half a mile to the East of the junction between the A307 and A309. If travelling from the East, Claygate Lane is the turning on the left immediately before the railway bridge. If travelling from the West, Claygate Lane is immediately after the second railway bridge though there is unfortunately, no right turn allowed from this direction.

THORNE MEMORIAL PARK MINIATURE RAILWAY

Address: Thorne Memorial Park, South Parade, Thorne, near Doncaster, S. Yorks.
Phone Nº: (01302) 842948 (Secretary)
Year Formed: 1996
Location of Line: Thorne Memorial Park
Length of Line: ¼ mile

Nº of Steam Locos: 2 (+ visiting locos)
Nº of Other Locos: 12
Nº of Members: Approximately 30
Approx Nº of Visitors P.A.: 1,400
Gauge: 5 inches and 7¼ inches
Web site: www.thornerailway.org.uk

GENERAL INFORMATION

Nearest Mainline Station: Thorne North (½ mile)
Nearest Bus Station: Bus stop outside the railway
Car Parking: Disabled parking only on site. Street parking and a public car park is nearby.
Coach Parking: Available nearby in the town centre
Food & Drinks: Light refreshments available

SPECIAL INFORMATION

The Railway is operated by volunteers from the Doncaster & District Model Engineering Society.

OPERATING INFORMATION

Opening Times: The first Sunday of the month from October to February, every Sunday and Bank Holiday Monday from Easter until the end of September and Wednesdays in August. Trains run from 12.00pm to 4.30pm.
Steam Working: Please check the railway's web site prior to visiting to see if steam is working on any given day. Alternatively phone 07751 486112. Please use this number only on operational days.
Prices: 40p per ride.

Detailed Directions by Car:
Thorne Memorial Park is situated in the centre of Thorne by the A614 just next to the Stainforth Keadby Canal. From the motorway exit the M18 at junctions 5 or 6 and follow the A614 or A1146 into Thorne.

THORNES PARK MINIATURE RAILWAY

Address: Thornes Park, Lawefield Lane, Wakefield, West Yorkshire	**N° of Steam Locos**: 7
Telephone N°: (01522) 800954 (Secretary)	**N° of Other Locos**: 4
Year Formed: 1952	**N° of Members**: 35
Location: Thornes Park, Wakefield	**Annual Membership Fee**: £3.00
Length of Line: ½ mile	**Approx N° of Visitors P.A.**: 45,000
	Gauges: 7¼ inches and 5 inches

GENERAL INFORMATION

Nearest Mainline Station: Wakefield Westgate (¾ mile)
Nearest Bus Station: Wakefield (1¼ miles)
Car Parking: Available on site
Coach Parking: Available on site
Souvenir Shop(s): None
Food & Drinks: None

SPECIAL INFORMATION

The railway is operated by members of the Wakefield Society of Model and Experimental Engineers. The group is non-profit making and all proceeds after operating costs are donated annually to the Mayor of Wakefield's chosen charity.

OPERATING INFORMATION

Opening Times: Sundays from Easter to October plus Saturdays and Bank Holidays depending on availability of manpower. Trains run from 1.00pm to 5.00pm. Also open for some other special events. Operation is dependent on weather conditions.
Steam Working: Generally whenever the railway is operating.
Prices: Adults 20p
Children 20p (free of charge for infants)

Detailed Directions by Car:
From All Parts: Thornes Park is located approximately 2 miles from Wakefield City Centre, just off the main Huddersfield to Wakefield road (A638).

TONBRIDGE MODEL ENGINEERING SOCIETY

Address: The Slade, Castle Grounds, Tonbridge, Kent TN9 1HR
Telephone Nº: (01892) 538415
Year Formed: 1944
Location: Castle Grounds, Tonbridge
Length of Line: ¼ mile

Nº of Steam Locos: 40
Nº of Other Locos: 1
Nº of Members: Approximately 100
Approx Nº of Visitors P.A.: 14,000
Gauge: 3½ inches and 5 inches
Web site: www.tmes.pwp.blueyonder.co.uk

GENERAL INFORMATION

Nearest Mainline Station: Tonbridge (1 mile)
Nearest Bus Station: Tonbridge (1 mile)
Car Parking: Available on site
Coach Parking: None
Food & Drinks: Available

SPECIAL INFORMATION

The Society has run a track at the present site since 1951 and since then facilities have been extended to include a steaming bay and turntable, passenger trollies, refreshment facilities and meeting room, store, and a well appointed workshop.

OPERATING INFORMATION

Opening Times: Saturday and Sunday afternoons throughout the Summer, weather permitting. Please contact the railway for further information.
Steam Working: Every operating day.
Prices: Free of charge but donations are accepted.

Detailed Directions by Car:
Exit the A21 Tonbridge Bypass at the junction signposted for Tonbridge South. Drive up the High Street, cross over the River Medway and turn left by the sign for the Swimming Pool. Follow the road round, turn left at Slade School and the car park for the railway is directly ahead.

VIABLES MINIATURE RAILWAY

Address: Viables Craft Centre,
The Harrow Way, Basingstoke, RG22 4BJ
Telephone Nº: None
Year Formed: 1976 (at current location)
Location of Line: Viables Craft Centre
Length of Line: 1,100 feet

Nº of Steam Locos: Members locos only
Nº of Other Locos: Members locos only
Nº of Members: Approximately 65
Approx Nº of Visitors P.A.: Not known
Gauge: 3½ inches and 5 inches
Web site: www.basingstoke-dmes.co.uk

GENERAL INFORMATION

Nearest Mainline Station: Basingstoke (2 miles)
Nearest Bus Station: Basingstoke (2 miles)
Car Parking: Free parking available on site
Coach Parking: Available
Souvenir Shop(s): Various shops at the craft centre
Food & Drinks: Available

SPECIAL INFORMATION

The railway is operated by volunteers from the
Basingstoke & District Model Engineering Society
and the current track at Viables Craft Centre opened
in 1979.

OPERATING INFORMATION

Opening Times: The railway runs on the first
Sunday of the month from March to October
inclusive and also in December, weather permitting.
Also a number of other special events – please check
the railway's web site for further details of these.
Trains run from 11.00am to 4.00pm.
Steam Working: Every operating day.
Prices: £1.00 per ride (two circuits of the track).

Detailed Directions by Car:
Viables Craft Centre can be found on the Southern side of Basingstoke, just minutes travel from the A30 and near
the A339 Alton Road and Junction 6 of the M3. The Centre is well signposted locally and is open throughout the
year with free entrance and car parking.

WESTON MINIATURE RAILWAY

Address: Marine Parade, Weston-super-Mare, Somerset	**N⁰ of Steam Locos**: 1
Telephone N⁰: (01934) 643510	**N⁰ of Other Locos**: 2
Year Formed: 1981	**N⁰ of Members**: None
Location of Line: Marine Parade	**Annual Membership Fee**: –
Length of Line: 900 yards	**Approx N⁰ of Visitors P.A.**: 20,000
Web site: westonmr.tripod.com	**Gauge**: 7¼ inches

GENERAL INFORMATION

Nearest Mainline Station: Weston-super-Mare
Nearest Bus Station: Weston-super-Mare
Car Parking: Available nearby on the seafront
Coach Parking: Available on the seafront
Souvenir Shop(s): Yes
Food & Drinks: Available

SPECIAL INFORMATION

This is a popular tourist railway running along the
Weston-super-Mare seafront.

OPERATING INFORMATION

Opening Times: Daily from Spring Bank Holiday
until September. Also open at weekends from
February to October.
Steam Working: Some Sundays.
Prices: Adult £1.50
        Child £1.50

Detailed Directions by Car:
From All Parts: The Railway is situated at the Southern end of the seafront in Weston-super-Mare. Follow the
brown tourist signs

WOKING MINIATURE RAILWAY

Address: Barrs Lane, Knaphill, Woking, Surrey GU21 2JW
Telephone Nº: (01483) 720801
Year Formed: 1989
Location of Line: Knaphill, Surrey
Length of Line: 1 mile

Nº of Steam Locos: 10
Nº of Other Locos: 6
Nº of Members: 110
Annual Membership Fee: £15.00
Approx Nº of Visitors P.A.: 15,000
Gauge: 7¼ inches
Web site: www.mizensrailway.org.uk

GENERAL INFORMATION

Nearest Mainline Station: Woking
Nearest Bus Station: Woking
Car Parking: 200 spaces available on site
Coach Parking: Available on site
Souvenir Shop(s): Yes
Food & Drinks: Available on running days

SPECIAL INFORMATION

The Railway is situated in a beautiful location admist 8 acres of woodland. In addition to over a mile of track, the railway has three stations, two signalboxes, a tunnel, a Roundhouse Engine Shed, a level crossing and authentic buildings.

OPERATING INFORMATION

Opening Times: Easter Sunday then every Sunday from May to September. Trains run from 2.00pm to 5.00pm. Santa Specials run on Sundays in December from 11.00am to 3.00pm.
Steam Working: Most operating days
Prices: Adult Return £1.50 – £2.00
          Child Return £1.50 – £2.00

Detailed Directions by Car:
From All Parts: Exit the M25 at Junction 11 and follow the A320 to Woking. At the Six Cross Roads Roundabout take the 5th exit towards Knaphill then turn left at the roundabout onto Littlewick Road. Continue along Littlewick Road crossing the roundabout before turning right into Barrs Lane just before Knaphill.

WOLDS WAY LAVENDER

Address: Wintringham, Malton, North Yorkshire YO17 8HW	**Nº of Steam Locos:** None as yet
Telephone Nº: (01944) 758641	**Nº of Other Locos:** 1
Year Formed: 2004	**Approx Nº of Visitors P.A.:** 30,000
Location of Line: Malton, N. Yorkshire	**Gauge:** 7¼ inches
Length of Line: 200 metres	**Web site:** www.woldswaylavender.co.uk

GENERAL INFORMATION

Nearest Mainline Station: Malton (6 miles)
Nearest Bus Station: Yorkshire Coastliner Bus Service runs between Leeds, Tadcaster, Malton & Scarborough. (Tel 01653 692556). Unfortunately, there is a half a mile walk from the bus stop.
Car Parking: Free parking available on site
Coach Parking: Free parking available on site
Souvenir Shop(s): Yes
Food & Drinks: Available

SPECIAL INFORMATION

Wolds Way Lavender operates one of the few working miniature railways in the country. The train is used to bring the Lavender in from the fields to the Distillery. The train also carries the logs to fire the still in addition to the passenger carriages that are used for train rides.

OPERATING INFORMATION

Opening Times: Daily from the first Sunday in February to the last Sunday in October. Open from 10.00am to 4.00pm and until 5.00pm from June to August. Train rides throughout the day.
Steam Working: None as yet though a steam loco is currently under construction.
Prices: £1.00 per ride.

Detailed Directions by Car:
Wolds Way Lavender is half a mile off the A64 York to Scarborough road on the Scarborough side of Malton. Look out for the Brown tourist signs for Wolds Way Lavender on the main road.

WOLVERHAMPTON & DISTRICT M.E.S.

Address: Baggeridge Country Park, Near Sedgley, Staffordshire	**Nº of Steam Locos**: 10
Telephone Nº: (01902) 842829	**Nº of Other Locos**: 5
Year Formed: 1986	**Nº of Members**: 52
Location: Baggeridge Country Park	**Approx Nº of Visitors P.A.**: Not known
Length of Line: Ground level line is a fifth of a mile, the raised track is 420 feet	**Gauge**: 3½ inches, 5 inches & 7¼ inches

GENERAL INFORMATION

Nearest Mainline Station: Wolverhampton (7 miles)
Nearest Bus Station: Sedgley (2 miles)
Car Parking: Available on site
Coach Parking: Available on site
Food & Drinks: Available

SPECIAL INFORMATION

The Wolverhampton & District Model Engineering Society operates the railway which runs through the Baggeridge Country Park. This was formerly the Baggeridge Colliery and part of the original Himley Estate of the Earls of Dudley. Since the closure of the Colliery, the site has been transformed into 150 acres of attractive country park.

OPERATING INFORMATION

Opening Times: Every other Sunday from April to September. Please phone the Secretary for more precise information. Trains run from 11.00am to 5.00pm.
Steam Working: Most operating days.
Prices: No charge but donations are accepted.

Detailed Directions by Car:
Take the A449 Wolverhampton to Kidderminster road then turn onto the A463 towards Sedgley. Baggeridge Country Park is just to the South of the A463 after approximately 2 miles and it is well-signposted from the road.

WORTLEY TOP FORGE MINIATURE RAILWAY

Contact Address: 3 Grange Road, Royston, Barnsley S71 4LD	**N° of Steam Locos**: Varies
Telephone N°: (01226) 728423	**N° of Other Locos**: Varies
Year Formed: Not known	**N° of Members**: Approximately 60
Location of Line: Top Forge, Wortley near Thurgoland in Sheffield	**Annual Membership Fee**: £15.00
Length of Line: ¼ mile	**Approx N° of Visitors P.A.**: Not known

Contact Address: 3 Grange Road,
Royston, Barnsley   S71 4LD
Telephone N°: (01226) 728423
Year Formed: Not known
Location of Line: Top Forge, Wortley
near Thurgoland in Sheffield
Length of Line: ¼ mile

N° of Steam Locos: Varies
N° of Other Locos: Varies
N° of Members: Approximately 60
Annual Membership Fee: £15.00
Approx N° of Visitors P.A.: Not known
Gauges: 7¼ inches and 5 inches
Web site: www.wortleymes.com

GENERAL INFORMATION

Nearest Mainline Station: Barnsley or Sheffield
Nearest Bus Station: Barnsley
Car Parking: Available on site
Coach Parking: Available on site
Souvenir Shop(s): None
Food & Drinks: Available in the Club house

SPECIAL INFORMATION

The railway is owned by the Wortley Top Forge
Model Engineers Society and runs through the
grounds of the Wortley Top Forge industrial
museum.

OPERATING INFORMATION

Opening Times: Sunday afternoons from Easter
until November.
Steam Working: Most operating days.
Prices: Donations are accepted

Detailed Directions by Car:
Wortley Top Forge is situated within 10 minutes drive of the M1 motorway. From the South: Exit the M1 at
Junction 35A and follow the A616 then A629 to Thurgoland; From the North: Exit the M1 at Junction 36 and
follow the A61 then A616 and finally the A629 to Thurgoland. Once in Thurgoland, the forge site is ½ mile to
the west of the traffic lights in the centre of the village.

WYTHALL MINIATURE STEAM RAILWAY

Address: The Transport Museum, Chapel Lane, Wythall, Birmingham, B47 6JX
Telephone Nº: (01564) 826471
Year Formed: 1980s
Location of Line: The Transport Museum, Wythall
Length of Line: 945 feet

Nº of Steam Locos: Members locos
Nº of Other Locos: Members locos
Nº of Members: Approximately 30
Approx Nº of Visitors P.A.: Not known
Gauge: 3½ inches, 5 inches & 7¼ inches
Web site: www.wythallsteamrail.co.uk

GENERAL INFORMATION

Nearest Mainline Station: Wythall (2 miles)
Nearest Bus Station: Birmingham (8 miles)
Car Parking: Available on site
Coach Parking: Available on site
Souvenir Shop: Yes (not specifically railway oriented)
Food & Drinks: Available

SPECIAL INFORMATION

The railway is operated by members of the Elmdon Model Engineering Society and is sited at the museum site of the Birmingham & Midland Omnibus Trust. See www.bammot.org.uk for details.

OPERATING INFORMATION

Opening Times: The Museum itself is open every weekend from Easter until the end of November. The railway operates on the following dates in 2007: 8th & 9th April; 6th, 7th, 27th & 28th May; 24th June, 26th & 27th August and 14th October.
Steam Working: Every operating day.
Prices: 50p per ride.
Note: An additional fee is charged for entrance to the Museum itself which is required to use the railway.

Detailed Directions by Car:
Wythall is situated on the A435 Alcester to Birmingham road near to Junction 3 of the M42. If travelling from the South, turn left at the roundabout upon reaching Wythall and the Museum is signposted from there. Turn right at this roundabout if travelling from the North.

ALSO AVAILABLE –

LITTLE PUFFERS

A Guide To Britain's Narrow Gauge Railways 2007/2008

£6.99

The new 3rd edition of **Little Puffers** is packed with information about Britain's top Narrow-gauge Railways and includes –

• **PHOTOS** • **DIRECTIONS** • **FARES** • **STEAMING DATES** • **CONTACT INFO**

...and much more. ***Priced just £6.99*** (UK post free)

Order from:

Marksman Publications, 72 St. Peters Avenue, Cleethorpes, DN35 8HU

Telephone (01472) 696226 Fax (01472) 698546 www.stillsteaming.com

ALSO AVAILABLE –

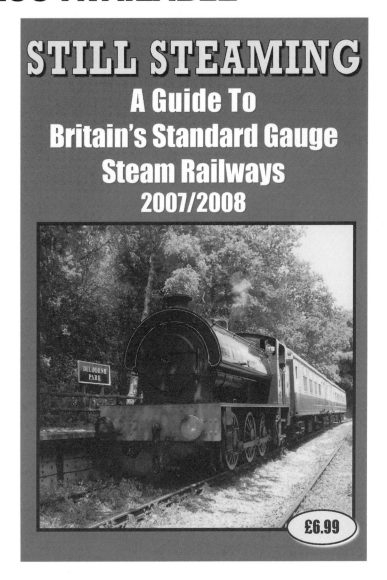

STILL STEAMING
A Guide To Britain's Standard Gauge Steam Railways
2007/2008

£6.99

The new 11th edition of **Still Steaming** is packed with information about Britain's top Standard-gauge Railways and includes –

• **PHOTOS** • **DIRECTIONS** • **FARES** • **STEAMING DATES** • **CONTACT INFO**

…and much more. ***Priced just £6.99*** (UK post free)

Order from:

Marksman Publications, 72 St. Peters Avenue, Cleethorpes, DN35 8HU

Telephone (01472) 696226 Fax (01472) 698546 www.stillsteaming.com